P9-DEC-316

Every Woman Can Be Adored

OTHER BOOKS BY MAXINE SCHNALL:

My Husband, The Doctor
The Broadbelters
The Wives Self-Help Program
Limits

Every Woman Can Be Adored

Maxine Schnall

Coward-McCann, Inc.
New York

Copyright © 1984 by Maxine Schnall
All rights reserved. This book, or parts thereof, must not be reproduced
in any form without permission. Published simultaneously in Canada by
General Publishing Co. Limited, Toronto.

Excerpt from the article "Baby Hunger" by Dr. Lois Leiderman Davitz
reprinted by permission of The McCall Publishing Company. Copyright
© 1981 by The McCall Publishing Company.

Library of Congress Cataloging in Publication Data

Schnall, Maxine
Every woman can be adored.

1. Love. 2. Self-confidence. 3. Courtship.
4. Success. I. Title.
HQ801.S437   1983   646.7'7   83–20903
ISBN 0–698–11267–9

Printed in the United States of America

Third Impression

Acknowledgments

Grateful acknowledgment is hereby given to the following people:

Thomas Ward Miller, who had the good sense to buy this book; Phyllis Grann, President and Publisher of G. P. Putnam's Sons, who gave the book its name and its future; Nancy Perlman, my talented and supportive editor; Harriet Blacker, who heads Putnam's publicity department; Andrea Bass and Audrey Cusson, also of Putnam's; Bill Adler, my agent; Sandra Drucker, who was there when I needed her; Marsha Sullivan and Hilarie Barsky, my "kitchen cabinet" at WCAU-AM; my mother, Clare Squires, and my dauthers, Ilene Schnall and Rona Schnall, who always provide encouragement and advice; and most of all, my husband, Larry, who proved conclusively to me that Every Woman Can Be Adored.

To my husband, Lawrence R. Mitnick

Contents

Introduction

The statement "Every woman can be adored" is not a lunatic claim; it's an assertion I make knowing full well how it feels to be on the losing end of love. Ten years ago when I was unhappily married, or even five years ago when I was unhappily single, I'd have snickered at a book title like this and wondered what drugs the author was doing. In those days I had little faith in anyone's chances for romantic success, least of all my own.

But then something happened that turned it all around. My last child went off to college, and I was utterly alone for the first time in my life—all forty-four years of it. As I paced the empty rooms of my house, I knew that I would have to change the course of my relationships or face being alone forever.

Like someone vowing to give up a life-threatening habit, I resolved that I would adopt a new strategy for finding happiness in love. No more would I put myself at the mercy of chance encounters or invest in a relationship that from the outset was obviously doomed to fail. Where would I have gotten, I mused, if I'd conducted my business affairs in such a haphazard laissez-faire fashion? Suddenly I saw the connection between success in love and success on the job! I realized that if I wanted to advance up the love ladder, I'd have to take control of my opportunities and implement my own objectives with the same courage, discipline, effort, and hard-nosed thinking that had brought me success in business.

The rest, as they say, is history. As I sit here counting my blessings—a husband who's everything I ever wanted in a man, a beautiful new home in Society Hill, a major diamond engagement ring, mementos of a honeymoon in Paris and the French Riviera, and all those other joys you fantasize about but assume will come to you only in your next life—I know that what I have to say about romantic success isn't Pollyanna. It *works*. There's no magic formula involved here, only a new way of looking at love, a way that says to women: Now that you've become sexually liberated, you must become emotionally liberated as well and learn to use your power to bring about the quality of love you want.

The principles set forth in this book will help you do that. This isn't a how-to book in the ordinary sense. I don't think anyone can tell you how to be lovable—what lines to say, how to act—and purport to make you irresistible to every man you meet. That kind of advice is dangerous. More than simple instructions, you need a *philosophy* of love to give you a handle on the subject.

What you'll find in *Every Woman Can Be Adored* is a philosophy of love not unlike the mind-set common to winners in other areas of life—business tycoons, champion athletes, etc. My philosophy dares to tell women that the ability to love can be mastered instead of merely experienced. It shows you how to take the kinds of principles and strategies that made it possible for our sex to attain success in the working world and apply them to the pursuit of happiness in relationships.

While *Every Woman Can Be Adored* speaks to the single woman of today, its message is valid for the married woman, too. Wives are notorious for not exerting their power in love as they should. Like prime examples of the Peter Principle, many have bungled their way to the top and are nervously wondering, What do I do now? If you're one of these, you certainly need to learn the new way of loving that I've espoused in this book—a way of loving that gives you control over your own choices.

The secret of success in any human endeavor is the will to win. How else can you activate the taste for victory except by rising above the fear of loss or by coming back from defeat? In love, disappointment is the best incentive. If *Every Woman Can Be Adored* does nothing more than inspire you to be encouraged rather than intimidated by visions of romantic bliss, it will have been enough.

Every Woman Can Be Adored

1

Lovemanship: A Method in Your Madness

*I*f you're one of those terminal romantics who believe that love is a happy accident ("Someday he'll come along, the man I love," etc.), this book is not for you. Put it down and keep waiting for one of Cupid's arrows to find a home in your heart. But don't blame me if you have a long wait.

If, on the other hand, you've noticed that nothing comes to those who only stand and wait except frustration, varicose veins, and creeping old age, read on. I'm here to tell you that with the right stuff in your quiver, you can beat Cupid at his own game. Cupid, don't forget, didn't have to contend with such phenomena as changing sex roles and the new sexual freedom and other complexities of modern life. You *do*. But once you have a *system* for dealing with the traps that are peculiar to love in our time, you can concentrate on the opportunities. And—equally important—as long as your opportunities find you *prepared* for them, you can't miss! Perhaps I sound unduly optimistic, but I know what worked for me.

It wasn't very long ago that I belonged to those legions of women who are bright, attractive, gainfully employed, and alone. At forty-six, I'd put in five years in the singles world after the breakup of a twenty-year marriage. I know some people adore being alone, and I say more power to them. Personally, I thought the single life left a lot to be desired— namely, a good man. I was convinced that "all the good ones are married," because the only unmarried ones I kept bumping into were definitely *not* good, at least for me.

In the summer of '79, I realized that my act was dreadfully in need of revision. I changed my attitude, buffed up my image to a high gleam, and mounted an aggressive search for the Right One. By January 1980, I'd found him. Larry is a year older than I am, tall and handsome, bright, successful, sexy, loving, sensitive, funny, generous, honorable, and the only man I could ever team up with on the Sunday *New York Times* crossword puzzle without coming to blows. If I'd sent God a requisition slip for the perfect partner, I couldn't have done better. (Forgive me the excesses of a woman in love.)

A year after we began dating, Larry and I decided to get married. The night we became engaged (New Year's Eve, 1981— what could be more romantic?), we kept telling each other, "I only wish I'd met you sooner. We could have been happy together all this time." A marvelous sentiment, but not true. Had I met Larry earlier, Right One though he is, we'd have clicked worse than a bad pair of false teeth. Why? Because I wasn't ready. I *thought* I was ready, since a relationship was something I wanted desperately. Desperation, however, is a whole different ball game from readiness—and a losing one. It wasn't until I'd given desperation the boot—ironically, by losing at love often enough to smarten up from my mistakes— that I was ready to win.

From the moment I met Larry, I sensed I was doing something right. I was attracted to him immediately but couldn't ignore two formidable obstacles to our relationship: We lived sixty miles apart from each other in different states, and he'd only been separated fifteen months and was enjoying his freedom to the hilt. And yet I wasn't intimidated. Instinctively, it seemed, I knew what to do and when to do it. (It wasn't instinct, really; it was the subliminal smarts.) I was candid about my life when it couldn't hurt me and cryptic when it could. I bluffed to make him jealous when he was cocky and told the truth when he needed to be reassured. I gave when he could handle it and held back when he couldn't. I took a stand when it mattered and overlooked when it didn't. I pursued when I had to outdistance the competition and hung loose when *he* was rounding the homestretch after *me*, and let myself be caught.

What I was doing, without being aware of it, was practicing the art of lovemanship—a name I've since come up with to describe loving with your head as well as your heart. No, lovemanship is not just a fancy new name for your grand-mother's coy, manipulative, and calculating wiles that sup-posedly went out with whalebone corsets. I'm not knocking your grandmother—it's entirely possible that she was playing with a fuller deck than many women are now. But that's not the issue. The point is, the savvy single woman of today, having grown a spine in recent years, wants to win at love without stooping so low to conquer that she can't straighten up again. Old-style manipulation—being a sexual tease, pre-tending to idolize him, threatening to throw yourself under a bus if he won't marry you—is, mercifully, a thing of the past.

But this doesn't mean that you have to come on with all the finesse of a Sherman tank. Being up front has its limits. You're not compromising your integrity, your equality, or your sub-scription to *Ms.* by recognizing that success in love requires skill, adroitness and delicacy of performance, and the ability to handle delicate and difficult situations artfully and diplo-matically (Webster's definition of *finesse*). Does artfulness in love strike you as outdated? Then let me ask you this: If lib-erated women have learned how to be brainy in the workplace and still be fully feminine, why can't they be brainy in love and still be fully liberated?

They can, obviously, or they ought to get out of the love game altogether and stick to earning a living. While we're on the subject, by calling love a "game," I don't mean to put it in the same category as Rubik's Cube. I'm of the opinion that

love soars above mathematical high jinks—or any other arbitrary game-playing for that matter. Impervious to poets and
scientists alike, love is, and always will be, I hope, one of life's
most profound, elemental, and sacred mysteries. It's also a lot
of fun.

It's the fun side of love that has been in a coma since we
turned it into a clinical case history. Who wants to know how
to "interact" with a man, or, worse yet, "confront" him? If you
don't enjoy each other, why bother? The trick is to have a
good time. It helps when you stop thinking about a Relationship as a life-or-death matter and get involved in the elements
of play that make love a game: the thrill of the chase, the
delicious sport of point-counterpoint, the sweet pleasure of
discovery. All other things being equal, you can bet your ring
finger that if you're giving him more fun and excitement than
anyone he's ever known, the bottom line will take care of itself.

There's another reason why the game theory applies to love,
and that brings us back to the wisdom of getting out in the
field rather than sitting home waiting for things to happen.
People who've studied games have shown that there's more to
winning than pure chance. Successful game players are continually measuring their options and making the most of them.
Whether it's blackjack or the relationship crapshoot, the players who walk off with the most chips are the ones who get a
high from healthy competition and can make intelligent decisions on the basis of incomplete information (only the Big
Dealer in the sky knows *everything*).

Sadly enough, many women break out in cold sweats when
they contemplate having to compete against other women for
a hard-to-get male. The prospect of engaging in a duel of wills
with various males, some hard-to-get, others too eager, doesn't
thrill them any either. This is where the game theory of love
comes in handy. If you take the attitude that, win or lose, the
playing is its own reward, competition becomes a challenge
rather than a cause for flop sweats. So what if you take your

lumps every once in a while? Mistakes, as I discovered, are the greatest little teachers in the world. The pearls of wisdom that make up the syllabus of lovemanship were strung together from a slew of mistakes—mine and other people's.

The love game, like the game of life itself, is a form of psychological combat. Ultimately, it's not your looks, charm, style, sexiness, or Cuisinart cookery that will see you through—although they're nice to have—but that intangible factor known as "self-confidence." When you decide that a particular man is worth it, you've got to hang in and tough it out. Somehow—and I'll get into how later—you've got to harden your Achilles' heel—let's say it's jealousy, anxiety, impatience, anger, submissiveness—and go for the big win with the supreme confidence of a Chris Evert executing a daring backhand shot. Staying on top of the situation, coolly and boldly, while you're playing out your options is what separates the women from the girls (and the winners from the losers) every time.

The Business of Love

More than any other game, winning at love most resembles success in business. Love and *business* in the same breath? Yes! But my frame of reference is not as cold and calculating as you might think. If anything, it's immensely human, assuming that by "human" we mean living and loving up to your fullest potential.

I'm not suggesting a balance-sheet mentality as the way to happiness in affairs of the heart; I'm merely pointing out that effective performance is effective performance, no matter where you do it. What's the difference if the focus of your activity is satisfaction on the job or happiness in a relationship? Although the worlds of work and love operate on disparate sets of assumptions, there's a basic similarity: Getting along well in either one requires a knowledge of what's out there and mastery of yourself in order to achieve the best mesh. What love and work have in common in today's world, with the dizzying new opportunities that have opened up for us in the bedroom and the boardroom, is this: *The most successful women are those who have a firm grasp of their personal power and how to use it.*

To some people, the word *power* still has those nasty old connotations of dominance, coercion, or restraint of the submissive that it acquired in the hands of macho men. But for women today, who are mainly concerned with power as a means of controlling *themselves, power* may best be defined as the capacity to implement choices or, in terms of results, the ability to make things happen. From whence cometh this ability? From the *perception* of it—what you see is what you get. As Herb Cohen explains in *You Can Negotiate Anything:* "Power is a mind-blowing entity. . . . If you think you've got it, then you've got it. If you think you don't have it, even if you have it, then you don't have it."

It's that simple. Whether it's the job market we're talking about or a relationship, the formula for success is the same: Call your own shots; don't depend on luck, fate, or the whims of others to do it for you—put *yourself* in the driver's seat. You may not want marriage at all, but simply a sexual friendship. No matter—let the choices be yours; don't be pushed along by someone else's goals. *You* be the one to decide what kind of man and what kind of relationship are best for you, and act on the basis of those decisions.

It's no secret that women understand the uses of personal power in the working world. They're familiar with the terminology—assume responsibility for your interests; exercise control over events; take charge of the situation—and they've applied these concepts zealously, often with stunning success. Yet these same women, who may be supremely competent and confident in their work, frequently lead love lives of not-so-quiet desperation.

I've been aware of this for a long time, but never more so than when I went on a cross-country author's tour with my last book. In city after city, the same thing happened. Not only did women in the studio audience inundate me after the show with laments about the Man Problem, but very often so did the interviewer herself!

Pat, for example, had barely finished our segment on the popular news and talk show she hosts in one of our country's top ten markets when she turned to me and asked beseechingly, "Where do you find men? I go to socials and stand around like an outcast while everyone else gets asked to dance except me. I've been divorced for twelve years and have a beautiful home in the suburbs, but it's like living in a cell. If I didn't have my fifteen-year-old son with me, I'd die of loneliness. *What's wrong with me?*"

Whatever it was, it certainly wasn't her looks. Tall and willowy, in her late thirties, with a lovely, sloe-eyed face, she was a knockout by anyone's standards. You could surmise that her glamorous job intimidated men; but there are just as many, perhaps more secure, men who are drawn to a woman *because* of her celebrity and all the plush trappings that go with it.

It seemed incongruous to me that a woman like Pat, who'd planned and pushed her way to an enviable position in a field as demanding as communications, had allowed herself to become so helpless in her quest for men. If only she'd approached romance in the same way she'd approached her work—with the same understanding of the rules of the game and how to strategize for success within those rules. Then, instead of retreating into isolation after a few rebuffs at singles dances, she'd have devised a new game plan for becoming more accessible to men who wouldn't be frightened off by her aura of success. Obviously, the dances Pat went to did not attract such men. More important, neither did her hangdog manner, so out of character for a gutsy woman of achievement. In pursuit of her dream job in the media, she'd had her fair share of rejections, but she hadn't let them discourage her or sap her belief in herself. Otherwise, she'd still have been in the secretarial pool typing up the news reports of the on-air talent.

Another bright professional, this one an insurance claims adjuster, confided to me after our interview that she was trying to learn how to live without love. Michelle, a sultry-looking blonde of thirty-six who had never married, kept a framed picture of her cocker spaniel on her desk in lieu of the usual family photos. She said that her seven-year relationship with a married businessman finally ended when he came knocking on the door of her apartment one day, divorce decree in hand, proposing marriage. "I knew right away that it would never work," Michelle said. "He wasn't intellectual or arty enough for me. I didn't like his friends or his life-style. He was exciting to me only as long as I was trying to get him away from another woman, but as soon as I had him—*pffft.*"

Michelle then launched into a harrowing description of her attempt to find a replacement for her former lover. *My God, there he is!* she said to herself one night as she found herself staring into the beguiling eyes of a bearded, stylishly dressed man sitting near her in a bar. They had a few drinks together, and Jim, as he was called, came across as a virile, outdoorsy type who loved cars and horseback riding. He owned a couple of horses and lived on a farm in a rural area where he could indulge his passion for riding.

That was all Michelle had to hear. A horse nut herself, she made a date with Jim for the weekend to go riding at his place in the country. Saturday morning, hot and sweaty as she shlepped her riding gear off the train (she was a city dweller and didn't own a car), Michelle was slightly disgruntled. Her mood wasn't helped any by the churchly atmosphere of Jim's place—reminders of Christ's agony on the cross were everywhere. Michelle was Jewish but prided herself on being ecumenical. She'd noticed the gold cross around Jim's neck when she met him and thought nothing of it. But this was a bit heavy.

On horseback, riding side by side with Jim through the sparkling, sunlit fields on that glorious summer day, Michelle found her spirits lifting. Later, showered, and relaxing around the house with Jim over drinks, Michelle couldn't wait to go to bed with him. It occurred to her that he'd been drinking too much (it seemed he was never *without* a drink when he wasn't on the back of a horse), but she attributed his growing surliness to lust.

Nothing in her experience prepared her for what came next. Jim refused to have sex with her! He teased and tantalized her excruciatingly and then turned her down cold. Humiliated, Michelle demanded an explanation.

Jim shrugged and said simply, "I can't stand a woman after I've slept with her."

The psychiatrist Michelle was impelled to see after this incident was sympathetic but appalled at her lack of common sense. He wanted to know why a hard-nosed investigator with Michelle's gift for observation hadn't caught on to Jim sooner. "You don't need me," he said half-jokingly. "Your cocker spaniel could tell you why it didn't work out with a used-car salesman who happened to be a religious fanatic with a drinking problem."

Women who are at or near the top of exciting professions are by no means the only ones afflicted with this strange personality split: thoroughly competent at work and thoroughly incompetent at love. While even the most gifted are prone, as Pat and Michelle illustrate, no one is immune. Office workers, nurses, schoolteachers, beauticians, barmaids, salespeople, factory workers—anyone engaged in a job (which includes full-time homemakers and students) is susceptible. It strikes young and old alike. It has nothing to do with the famous population imbalance between men and women or other sociological trends. *It is a habit of mind.*

Statistics don't tell the story; experience does. If I'd listened to the numbers (over a million more single women than men between the ages of 30 and 54 . . . two women for every man in the 40–44 age group, etc.), I'd have erased myself from the picture a long time ago. Considering my age, income, and status, I'd have thought that "landing" a man like Larry was about as likely as landing on the moon without a space shuttle. And that's exactly how likely it *would* have been had I continued on my initial course. What turned the tide for me was not that marriageable men suddenly became more available, but that I became aware of my power to act in my own best interests in love. And I've seen women of every stripe—from professionals earning $60,000 a year to clerks earning $6,000—effect this same dramatic change in their romantic fortunes when they changed themselves.

The current "marriage squeeze" is real. In the age range when most first marriages occur, women do outnumber men by 11 percent because of past fluctuations in the birthrate. However, help is on the way. By the mid-1980s, the direction of the "marriage squeeze" will have reversed—as a result of the declining birthrate in the 1960s, *there will be more young men than women* in the age range when most people enter their first or only marriage.

Now for the bad news. Women who are unskilled at intimacy or so afraid of it that they deliberately pick impossible partners—like Michelle, the horseback-riding journalist—won't fare any better at the love game when the male players outnumber the women.

Why do women who perform capably in other areas of their lives fumble in love? Because they think love is beyond their control. In their personal lives, they still feel compelled to relinquish their initiative to men as the more powerful sex, and they confuse being in love with being blown away (which either excites them beyond belief or scares the hell out of them, depending on their particular preference). In any case, they're victims of the myth of love-as-lightning—a bolt that strikes suddenly and of its own accord. It seems incongruous to them to act as if they had a hand in the matter. They won't exercise their right to choose their opportunities carefully, or to push or pull back at will, because they're afraid they'll chase men away if they assert their power in a straightforward fashion. Yet, that's the very thing desirable men find most attractive!

It doesn't matter whether you buy my game or business analogies or not—you can think of love in terms of weight control, if that helps. The important thing is that you perceive love as a *process*, a series of actions or changes leading toward a desired result, the mastery of which is always well rewarded. The reward isn't your dream man necessarily (although it could be); it's deliverance from floundering, a sense of direction and purpose that will sustain you in hard times. I've seen too many women go at love blindly, spinning their wheels and suffering needless heartache, not to believe in management-by-objectives.

In my own case, it was only after I'd "come home" to Larry that I could see the grand design implicit in my twisted route. I know now the terrors and humiliations I could have spared myself (and which I hope to spare you) if I'd had a clearer vision of my goal and how to reach it and understood the rules and secrets of each rite of passage. The whole meaning of the feminist revolution is that women should be aware of their options and plan for them, and I submit to you that this is true in love no less than it is in all of life.

If you've consistently fouled out at love because of your haphazard, catch-as-catch-can approach, you might start worrying that you're more neurotic or less lovable than women in good relationships. Give yourself a break. You'd be amazed how your fears and doubts and even some of your less endearing qualities (and who doesn't have them?) pale to insignificance when you've found the right partner. Just getting a handle on some pleasant dating experiences goes a long way.

I've discovered that insight without acting on it is as useless as a frozen bank account. Mine is a course of action. It retraces and redesigns the path that many women, unaware of their personal power, have taken in search of the perfect (meaning committed) relationship. Starting out with the initial "crazy period" of indiscriminate sex and going through stages of progressively deepening awareness and strength in relationships with men, it's a path that leads ultimately to self-discovery.

When I first began writing this book, I thought of calling it *From Sex to Love*, a sequence of events that clearly puts the cart before the horse. The reason I toyed with this topsy-turvy title is that most people today follow this reverse pattern in romance: They couple first and, hopefully, become a couple later. This development could very well win the humanitarian award for ending sexual frustration, but it has created another problem, which is shaping up as the dilemma of our age: how to turn a sexual affair into a loving relationship?

While you shouldn't underestimate it, sexual attraction can be a red herring of the worst order. It can divert your mind from the heart of the matter and lead you to believe you've got the makings of a relationship when what you have is a cause for unmet hopes.

Sex also has a dangerous habit of backfiring on women who haven't been trained to play around with it as guardedly as men. Forcing yourself to be cool about sex against your will has its dangers, too. A relationship cast in a casual framework is often set that way in stone—it will resist to the death any later attempt on your part to shift it toward commitment. Here again, you must learn how to engage in sex as effectively as possible, but always in the service of your own objectives.

I'm not going to bore you in this book with long discussions about the nature of love. I couldn't tell you what love is any more than I could describe the color blue to a blind man— you know it when you see it. The one thing we can probably all agree on is that being in love is a kind of insanity. If it is madness, then that's all the more reason why we need some rules to guide us when we're under the influence. Crazy doesn't necessarily mean suicidal. In love, it's best to be crazy like a fox, as the saying goes.

I've often thought it strange that the women who are as passionate as a triple-X-rated movie—the ones who deserve to be lucky in love—are generally the poor souls who get themselves behind the worst eight ball. If you're one of those, my guess is that you're suffering from delusions of *glandeur*—those off-the-wall fantasies induced by passion (or that old bugaboo, desperation) that make us pick the most god-awful partners. You may even think you're being very *au courant*, bouncing from bed to bed on a roll of dead-end relationships. My dear, get with it! Putting yourself on the short end of the stick in romance is strictly old hat, no more contemporary than Madame Butterfly. Satisfaction is the sign of the times, as well as the epitome of romance. If there's anything romantic about being exploited, abused, rejected, taken for granted, or just plain unhappy, I've yet to find it. And believe me, you're not going to find it either if you insist on bumbling along without a method in your madness or hiding out in your room waiting for the Right One to fall through the transom.

I've already told you that my story has a happy ending. It's a bit of a miracle, actually, in view of the sorry start I got off to. But I don't blame myself for that, and neither should you if you feel that life Out There is the pits. For years, all of the popular advice on how to be sexually single has been geared to the adventurous, catch-as-catch-can type who's looking to get bludgeoned to death in bed by a handsome stranger. That's why I'm writing this book. I want to let you in on the way love *is*, not the way they say it is. The whole loaf, passion *and* love, can be yours—why *not* you?—but you have to face the facts and go after the package with your head on straight.

Now please don't get defensive and tell me that you can't learn from OPM (other people's mistakes), that you have to make your own. That's worse than the one about the genius who thought he should test the water for poison by drinking it first. Granted, you might want to make a few blunders on your own simply for the sake of originality, but most of them are in the poisoned-water category. Save your time and energy for something pleasurable. Besides being antiquated and un-romantic, losing needlessly *hurts*.

A word of caution before I proceed with the course. Not even the cleverest strategies nor the most brilliant ploys and techniques will fan love into being where the sparks don't exist. Readiness on either person's part can be negotiated sometimes, but rightness never can (see chapter 7, "The Right One"). Given a little fine tuning, if you're not basically right for each other, take your tennis shoes off and go home. Remember, if you win the game, you get the prize.

What follows then is not a treatise on how to get a man, which any woman who's warm and breathing can easily do. The subject we're addressing here is a far more challenging one: how to love and be loved the way you've always wanted—but didn't think you could.

2

Running Scared

*Y*ou're sitting at the bar in Maxwell's Plum feeling very sorry for yourself. You've just come off a yearlong relationship with a flaky, egocentric lawyer whose temper tantrums made you fear for your life. Before that, you had a brief but intense affair with a deceptively charming alcoholic you met—where else?—at another bar.

Sipping your Chablis slowly to make it last, you look around you and wonder why God has singled you out for such a gruesome fate. The few men here who could be considered remote possibilities are so aloof and indifferent (because they know they're in demand) that they appear to be on loan from a waxworks. Who *needs* this? you ask yourself. You feel you have a lot to offer a man. Why should you be sitting here like a bag lady in disguise, begging to be saved from oblivion by some conceited bore?

You have all but given up hope when suddenly you notice a good-looking man smiling at you in a most inviting way. You smile back, and the next thing you know he's standing beside you, looking for all the world like—gasp—Warren Beatty. Incredibly, he even sounds like Warren Beatty. In a voice pulsating with snob and sex appeal, he asks, "Don't you hate places like this?"

You stare at him, astonished that he's so perceptive. Before you can reply, he tells you that he has been observing you ever since you walked in, impressed by your presence and class as soon as he saw you. You thank him graciously, wondering if you're hallucinating, and manage to exchange a few pleasantries. When he asks you if you'd like to join him for dinner at a marvelous little Italian restaurant in SoHo, you accept with unrestrained joy. Imagine! Minutes ago you were in the depths of despair, and now a glittering opportunity is unfolding before you like the gates to the Taj Mahal.

The next five hours fly by with the crazy momentum of a dream. Over a delectable veal dish and goblets of wine, your conversation ranges across a broad spectrum of topics from low-carbohydrate diets to the rigors of dating. You find out that he's forty-one, does something with computers, jogs, plays tennis, reads the best books, cooks five-minute gourmet meals in a wok, loves movies and plays with substance, and lives in a delightful converted loft that, as luck would have it, is only a few blocks away. He has never married, but not, he quickly assures you, because he's unwilling; he simply has never found a woman with the depth and compassion he requires.

He has you absolutely mesmerized. You feel drawn to him by a magnetic pull. You're touched by his combination of worldliness and little-boy vulnerability. A feeling is welling up inside you that here at last is a man you can love, a caring man who will love you back, share his life with you, and always be in your corner. You realize that you've had this feeling before, and it was always dead wrong. But this time, you tell yourself, it's different. It *has* to be different. The thought of spending the rest of your life looking for men in bars is enough to make you want to switch from Chablis to cyanide on the rocks.

When he takes your hand, looks longingly into your eyes, and mentions something about going back to his place, you feel yourself begin to melt. You know you're rushing things, but the attraction is certainly there. Besides, you figure, a guy like this will never call you again if you turn him down. Why should he when every other woman in the city, to hear him tell it, is dying to get in his pants? So what if no one has managed to catch him up till now? You see that as a challenge. It annoys you that he's somewhat glib and fussy and arrogant, but you're still willing to gamble. Don't they all say you have to take risks? You know what to do: Get him hooked on you first, and you'll worry about the soft spots later.

His loft is just like him—done up in exquisite taste and terribly seductive. By this time you're euphoric on wine and passion, but you feel obliged to tell him that you have some misgivings. He understands perfectly and says exactly the right things to allay your doubts.

"I'm not interested in a one-night stand," he assures you earnestly. "I want intimacy, a real relationship. I've been waiting to find someone who turns me on totally the way you do—someone I can love and love and love."

He takes you in his arms and kisses you with the utmost tenderness, as if to express what he means without words.

You get the message. You smoke some grass with him, and the last vestige of caution slips away.

As soon as he begins to make love, you realize you've made a mistake. He's experienced all right, but his heart is elsewhere—he's as detached and mechanical as a keypunch operator. Competitive down to his very toenails, he's determined to wring pleasure out of you, not for your sake, God forbid, but to prove to himself (who else matters?) that he can do the job.

Afterward, you're lying next to him, searching for something to say. Suddenly he breaks the terrible silence between you and starts talking about Helen, the tragic love of his life. Helen is the only woman in the world he could ever feel anything for, but she wants no part of him. They lived together for six months and were constantly at each other's throat until Helen finally moved out. That was a year ago. He used to phone her every day, alternately screaming at her for leaving him and begging her to come back, but now she's dating others and won't take his calls.

He launches into a recital of Helen's virtues—"Helen is the best-looking woman in New York . . . Helen has an IQ of 160-plus . . . Helen jogs ten miles like it's a city block"—that both infuriates and mystifies you. Why didn't he hang on to this prize package, you'd like to know, when he had her? But then the answer occurs to you: He's the type who can love a woman only after she's gone.

You know there's nothing in this for you, so you get dressed and tell him you want to go home. He doesn't give you an argument. You get the feeling he's as glad to be rid of you as you are to leave.

Riding home in the cab, you're so angry you want to scream. That phony, self-serving creep! You'd like to strangle him for hitting on you like that when he's still hung up on another woman. You've never seen anyone take a cheaper shot in all your life. But that's not the worst of it, you realize miserably.

He wasn't even good in bed.

The preceding vignette, with minor variations, is true. It's a composite of countless incidents that have happened to just about every lovelorn woman who ever set foot in a singles bar. Despite the difference in details, the horror stories all follow the same general pattern: Woman flashes on hot-blooded man and gets burned.

It would be easy to deduce from these experiences that singles bars are to be avoided like a swarm of killer bees. But that deduction is misleading. I personally know of at least four women who are happily married to men they met in singles bars, and countless others (including myself) who were introduced to their partners through a platonic singles-bar contact. It's possible to meet a viable man *anywhere*, even in the mental institution where you both happen to be working. It's not the place but what you do after you get there that counts.

Admittedly, singles bars do have some murderous liabilities. There's the well-known "meat market" atmosphere that's geared to the youngest and the flashiest rather than the best and the brightest. There's the element of boredom when you have nothing else to do except drink and look around furtively. And worst of all, of course, there's the undesirability of many of the men singles bars tend to attract—mostly double-dealing marrieds out for a sexual fling, but also other unsavory types not suited for a self-respecting single woman who wants a serious relationship (a rundown appears later).

Pestholes though they may be, I still maintain that it's the *attitude of the women* looking for men in bars that gets them into trouble rather than the nature of the bars themselves. The fact is that discerning women, regardless of their age or looks, have used singles bars to their advantage. But the woman who is running scared is headed for disaster whether the man in question is a no-good bar pickup or an absolute gem handed to her through a white-gloved introduction.

Actually, while you're in the running-scared stage, you're better off making your mistakes with specimens from the singles-bar subculture rather than blowing your chances with someone who has real potential. To flop when you're playing summer stock in Peoria is hardly the same as bombing out on Broadway.

Now let's go back to our opening vignette, a study in the perils of running scared, and analyze step by step the faulty moves that led our heroine (that's you) astray.

Remember what propelled you into the bar in the first place? All those *ecchy* feelings anyone has after an affair has ended— loneliness, self-pity, fear, anger, disappointment, and a burning impatience to find a new partner. Such urgency does not make for good judgment, which is something you can't be without *ever*—especially when you're attempting to measure your options on a playing field as perilous as the bar scene.

Your first mistake, then, was going back into action prematurely, without giving yourself time to heal (you wouldn't expect Chris Evert to take to the court with her arm in a sling, would you?). This, I must quickly explain, is probably the commonest mistake of all. Instead of recovering from a bummer, most people start frantically hunting for a quick replacement while their judgment is still on hold. Typically, they hit the singles bars and dances with a manic intensity. Or they go on a dialing-for-dates telephone binge, calling up ex-lovers (even if the relationship ended horribly), acquaintances who have never been more than friends (and should stay that way), and anyone they ever said hello to. (Incidentally, if you should *receive* an out-of-the-blue phone call from an ex-lover, platonic friend, or nodding acquaintance, don't be fooled by his extraordinary interest in you; he's running scared after a spat with his girlfriend and wants to use you as a pacifier until he goes back to her.)

Had you gone to Maxwell's Plum that night as a spectator rather than a player, you could have spared yourself some grief. You'd have been content with conversation only, reserving decisions about dating and sex until you felt more competent to make them. It's a funny thing about choices—when you think you're running out of them, that's the time to be choosier than ever. To pull out of a slump, you've got to scratch for new options like a tigress but examine them *very carefully*. Since your morale is low, you have to compensate for your heightened vulnerability with the kind of discipline you normally reserve for a crash diet.

Hence, when that mouth-watering Warren Beatty look-alike approached you (let's call him Warren for fun), you should have forced yourself down from those delicious flights of fantasy and considered the facts, ma'am, just the facts. For example, any man of forty-one who says he has never married because he hasn't found a woman good enough is telling you something: He's trouble; solid, enduring attachments are not his specialty. Never mind that Warren had the looks and life-style of the man of your dreams; his success in avoiding commitment should have tipped you off that there was less here than met the eye.

There's nothing wrong with giving a man in his forties (not any older) the benefit of the doubt if he hasn't found that elusive someone. Maybe he *has* been waiting just for you. If he has, he should be thrilled to wait a little longer and savor the pleasure of your company. He should want to *woo* you, not lure you into bed in a headlong hurry. Yes, it's possible that he's avid to bed you down because he's genuinely attracted to you. But he won't *insist* on sex the first night unless the act of having sex with someone—for physical release, to relieve anxiety, to score status points, to retaliate for being dumped—means more to him than you do. The big rush is not flattering; it's suspect.

A man who's clever about the chase will do a turnabout so that the woman becomes the pursuer and he the pursued. Warren, for example, presented himself as a world-beater whose only difficulty with women was turning them away. He gave you the impression that unless you got into the running fast, you wouldn't have a prayer—a "limited offer" pitch favored by many salesmen. Because his options seemed so much greater than your own, you bowed out of all responsibility for the encounter and relinquished the choice to him.

Let's review your options as you saw them in your panic-stricken state: (1) Decline Warren's offer to sleep with him that night and never hear from him again, and (2) sleep with him and try to hook him into a relationship through sex. Meekly accepting the role of the pursuer, you grabbed at the second option—a long shot—and psyched yourself into it with that familiar pep talk about how you have to take risks.

And that, my friend, was your biggest mistake. Everyone knows that you can't get anywhere in life without taking risks, but only the winners know *how* to take them. The question is, what are the probabilities? What makes one option a *preferred risk*, in other words, over one with a predictably poor return?

When you're dealing with a man on the make who has put you in the position of the pursuer, you can count on this as an almost universal law (one of Maxine's Maxims, if you wish): *The path of least resistance is always the poorer risk.* By "least resistance" I mean acquiescing more out of fear than unalloyed desire. Specifically, it means jumping into bed with a man right away not because you're wild for him but because you're afraid not to. No matter how you try to hide it, your yellow streak invariably stands out to a would-be lover like Pac-Man running for his life. It's an open invitation to consume you on the spot (or more slowly, if the man is so inclined).

What should you have done in your encounter with Warren? Your *preferred* risk was not to sleep with him. It's the risk of rejection we're talking about here, and rejection by a man after you've had sex with him hurts a lot worse than if you haven't. Suppose you'd turned Warren down and, as feared, never heard from him again. What was to stop you from calling him? Not a thing. Since you didn't cross the dividing line between friendliness and total exposure of yourself, you had nothing at stake except a gracious and very casual invitation (your brother's wife gave you this pair of theater tickets; would he like to go?).

By this maneuver you've put him on notice that you're interested in him *on your terms*, as a grown-up woman capable of doing the pursuing when *she* wants to, not when she's pushed into it by a man whose motives aren't known. You've shown him that you're not some spineless creature he can bend out of shape to accommodate his purposes, but rather a spunky lady who has clearly defined intentions of her own—an intriguing match for the Helens of this world. If all you get for your trouble is a firm turndown, what've you lost? You've uncovered his true feelings with a phone call, not your sacred honor.

The Sexual Hook

Sleeping with a man on the first meeting, as many women will testify, does not preclude going on to develop a deeply satisfying, committed relationship of lengthy duration. But don't let these women fool you. They're either exceedingly intuitive or exceedingly lucky or both. They jumped into bed with men who, as it turned out, happened to be right for them *personally*, not just sexually. But the chances of their being *wrong* were staggering.

A spectacular sexual connection with a man tells you very little about him except that he's good in bed. Not only is it no indication that the man will be as well matched for you out of bed as he is in, but you can't even guarantee on the basis of his magnificent lovemaking that he has the capacity to care for you at all. That's why the sexual hook must be used with the utmost discretion. You need time—how much time depends on his willingness to talk and the keenness of your perceptions—in order to find out who this man is and what he's up to. Only men who are up to no good will balk at a leisurely process of discovery. Exercise the public's right to know.

Unless a man is an out-and-out scoundrel, he'll usually level with you about (or at least not try to conceal such matters as) an existing wife or girlfriend, raw emotional wounds, drug abuse, kinky sex habits, psychotic tendencies, no money, imminent deportation, and other insuperable drawbacks. And I mean *insuperable*. Good sex, even great sex, won't make the slightest dent in them. If the sexual hook works on a man who's a bad risk, it'll hook him with his problems intact.

What about the man whose only problem—and it's not so only—is a fear of commitment? Can the wonders of sex turn him around? It all depends on the severity of his disease. If he's a *curable commitmentphobe*—one who wants to play the field temporarily—he has possibilities; and sex, as we'll see later, just might be your trump card. *Incurable commitmentphobes* are those who've never sustained a long-term committed relationship or who are going through the intensive-care period of recovery from one (which could take anywhere from a few months to a lifetime). They are, as the name suggests, hopeless. You can grab their attention with the sexual hook, but you can never engage them completely.

Not every woman wants or needs a committed relationship, and in that case a phobe may be perfect for her. But many women pretend not to want commitment when they really do. I know of no greater single cause of romantic heartache than when a man who has given a woman every reason to believe that he *won't* marry her—doesn't. Invariably, it's the woman who has set herself up for this rejection by masking her real objectives or not believing the man's. One young woman I know lived with an avowed phobe for two years, proclaiming all the while that she didn't want to get married. Then she talked him into it (or so she thought), and was devastated when he bowed out of the relationship one week before their wedding date.

Let that be a caution to you. If you're looking for a serious, high-quality relationship that *could* lead to permanence, PAY ATTENTION. Don't ignore the early warning signs of intractable commitment phobia and plunge ahead anyway, hoping sex will effect a miracle cure. Listen to what he says ("I don't want to get tied down" . . . "All I want is a fun relationship" . . . "I'm not giving up my freedom" . . . or words to that effect) and *believe* him. In your eagerness to hook him, don't wait until after you've thrown that first harpoon to find out that you're playing with Moby Dick.

It's neither possible nor desirable to discover everything about a man before going to bed with him; spontaneity and risk-taking have their place, and people do change. But if throwaway sex is demeaning to you, when you're running scared you must discipline yourself not to make irrational choices born of desperation. With any man you've just met anywhere—in a bar, on the beach, in class, at work, at a party, on a blind date—check the tendency we all have at such times to act in haste and repent in leisure. (Panicky women spend less time, on the average, picking a bed partner than they do buying a dress—and a dress can't give you herpes!)

Use the technique that made Ted Williams one of the greatest baseball hitters of all time—*slow that pitch down.* Don't let yourself be crowded. Take that extra fraction of time to see all the angles—from *your* position, not the pitcher's—before you decide to swing.

Sexual encounters aren't sexist—they won't discriminate against a woman unless she asks for it by acting like a member of the weaker class. You have the same right as a man to take what you need from sex when it's offered. But *know* what you need.

Consider the case of Laura, a quietly assertive, very competent thirty-seven-year-old administrative assistant. She'd been separated from her husband five months when the urgency of her physical drive propelled her into a bar where she cold-bloodedly singled out a man for a one-night sexual excounter. "I had no feeling for this person," Laura remembers, "and I was worried that I'd feel guilty. But I got up four or five hours later without any compunction and said, 'See you.' "

When the man called her afterward, Laura told him very frankly that he was great sexually but that they had nothing else in common and he'd be wasting his time. "I'd always characterized that as a male attitude," she says, "but I needed sex so badly that it was a necessity. The encounter was a confidence-builder for me because I felt I had satisfied him. It got me over the hurdle of the first postdivorce sexual experience, and that's enough to scare you to death. I think half of it is 'I shouldn't, but I want to,' and the other half of it is 'Will I perform? Will I satisfy this man?' It took me a long time to realize that I was entitled to satisfaction, too."

In the interests of fair play, I think it best that you warn a man beforehand (as they so often gallantly warn us) that your intentions aren't serious. If he disbelieves your caveat or construes it as a challenge—as he most probably will—you can't be held responsible for false labeling.

Regardless of who plays which role, the dynamics of sexual encounters never vary. The *consumers*—those who want sex as an end in itself—can get a morale boost from it and not feel cheated if a deeper relationship never materializes. But the *seekers*—the ones who want more than physical release—may find that meaningless sex will obstruct them from getting what they want by sapping their confidence. When A, who wants an attachment through sex, meets B, who wants sex without getting attached, the encounter is going to leave A hungrier for an attachment than before—and feeling used and abused to boot.

As if your own insecurities weren't bad enough, your last shred of confidence and judgment can get buried when you're out in the field by that unnerving propaganda about the man shortage (nicely perpetuated, I might add, by men who often have nothing else going for them *except* numerical scarcity). The numbers game is tough, but there's such a thing as affirmative action. Beating the odds against them in a world skewed in favor of men is nothing new to women. When they're motivated, they can do it—ask any female lawyer, doctor, police officer, manager, or other woman happily holding down a "male" job.

A faulty relationship search can take you to places where there are so few men that even the most unthinkable ones start looking good. In the land of the blind, as someone once said, the one-eyed man is king. But don't generalize about the whole territory from one bad locale, and don't be reduced to cuddling up in bed with a Cyclops if that's not your style.

Most women I know who lowered their standards and picked men they didn't really want—the "safe" ones who wouldn't reject them—got rejected by the men eventually anyway! It's that old thing about being overqualified for the job. Seek your own level. Like the job market, the relationship market has a constant rate of "unemployment," but there are always a number of good "jobs" going begging. The path of least resistance won't lead you to them—that's the shortest distance between desperation and a dead end.

3

A Trap Is Not an Opportunity in Disguise

I told you at the very beginning of this book that the art of lovemanship hinges on knowing the difference between a trap and an opportunity. One thing a trap *isn't* is an opportunity in disguise. It may look like an opportunity, it may talk like an opportunity, it may make love like an opportunity—but it doesn't offer any room for advancement.

A relationship doesn't have to end in a hoped-for commitment to justify its existence; it may entail a loss worth suffering again for the gain. But there's a certain kind of relationship that provides no gain other than its instructive value—you know not to repeat this number again. This is a trap. It raises great expectations and delivers sharp disillusionment, and it comes to a predictably bad end that the means don't validate. The problem is that there are some men who want so much or can give so little that engaging with them is not worthwhile.

Walking into a trap occasionally isn't fatal, but doing it repeatedly is something to be avoided. When you consistently misplace your confidence in men who can't love, your own capacity to love is diminished. You either become more desperate, which in turn leads to greater disillusionment, or you begin drifting toward isolation.

To help you recognize some of the more dangerous traps you might come across when you're running scared, herewith are some profiles of the Six Least-Wanted Men.

1. The Lounge Lizard

A slick, smooth-talking womanizer, stylishly dressed and usually good-looking although slightly jaded around the edges,
the Lizard likes to hang out at singles bars because that's where
the action is (our friend Warren, who appeared in the preceding chapter, is a prime example). He's sophisticated—he
subscribes to *Cuisine*, speaks psychobabble, skis at Killington,
knows a Burgundy from a Bordeaux—but there's something
hollow about his charm. Frequently witty and clever and fast
with a phrase, he's also emotionally shallow and self-absorbed.
You're a prop for his routine, and he seldom asks you anything
about yourself except as an afterthought.

One of the Lounge Lizard's favorite ploys is to ingratiate
himself with his "openness," candidly revealing the most intimate details about himself soon after meeting you. You can
always tell from his well-timed delivery (bombshell
. . . pause . . . questioning look) that he's doing this for effect.
For example, don't get undone if he confides in the above
manner that he cries uncontrollably after orgasm. This is not
to show you how vulnerable he is—it's to whet your appetite.

Watch out for this man! He's an experienced heartbreaker
who's constitutionally incapable of caring for a woman after
he has her. A subspecies of commitmentphobe, the Lounge
Lizard shares the phobe's aversion to commitment and goes
him one worse. While the phobe is often unwittingly cruel to
women, the Lizard is intentionally sadistic. He's the type of
man who, moments after making uninhibited love to you, will
throw you out of his bed and send you packing (without even
giving you cab fare) because he's going to a party and doesn't
want you tagging along. Or, while you're still in his bed recovering from an energetic session of lovemaking, he'll take a
phone call from another woman and engage in a long, lan-
guorous conversation filled with sexual innuendos and come-

ons. The Lizard, bless his reptilian heart, will stop at nothing to demean you by playing on your jealousies and making you feel like a persona non grata.

Let me give you one brief incident to prove my point. Ingrid, a Nordically attractive twenty-six-year-old advertising copywriter, was reeling from a broken romance with an Israeli law student when she succumbed to Gil's literate and sophisticated charms. Gil was a divorced, middle-aged movie critic and man-about-town whom Ingrid met through her work (Lizards haunt lounges, but they can turn up anywhere). Two weeks into their affair, Gil, in typical Lizard fashion, invited Ingrid out one night and told her to pick him up at his apartment (it's a mark of the Lizard's arrogance never to pick you up; he expects you to do all of the heavy lifting).

Gil was in his bathrobe when he greeted Ingrid at the door, ushered her into his apartment, and blandly introduced her to two other woman guests she'd never seen before. The women smiled awkwardly at Ingrid, looking as tense and combative as a couple of cats arching for a fight. These were clearly not visiting cousins from Winnetka, but two aspiring girlfriends of Gil's who were waiting to audition for the part. Ingrid demanded an explanation. Gil coolly told her that he thought it would be "fun" if they had some company that night, implying that Ingrid would have to get in line if she wanted a crack at him. Ingrid, to her everlasting credit, decided the game wasn't worth the candle. She knew a trap when she saw one. "I'm sorry I can't stay, Gil," she said, moving toward the door. "There's not enough of you to go around."

Ingrid got out in time, but I can't tell you how many other women have endured unspeakable humiliation and debasement before they finally caught on: The Lizard, for all his inviting charm and sad-eyed preoccupation with fantasies of ideal love, is totally inaccessible.

What makes a Lizard crawl? Arousing the envy and admiration of others by possessing a desirable woman—and then cruelly cutting her down. A Lizard doesn't relate to you, he *wears* you. As much as he's out to scissor you to size, he also wants to show you off. He's obsessed with physical beauty. He worries about high cheekbones, shiny teeth, and sleek legs because these are the things that other people see. Your tiniest flaws will become repugnant to him in time. A Lizard once confided to me that he dropped a brainy, beautiful woman he thought he loved, because her hair didn't look as pretty on some days as it did on others!

There's no pleasing a Lizard. Should your body pass muster with him, he'll discover qualities of mind and soul to criticize. Besides being supremely status-conscious about women, the Lizard has another motive for demanding perfection: He knows he'll never find it and will thus be spared ever having to make a commitment. You exist for him only as a basis for comparison—you're no better than anyone he's had and not as good as someone he might meet.

Since you can't prove to the Lizard that you're good enough for him, why engage with him at all? You can't develop your lovemanship skills with someone this scaly, or even have more than forgettable sex. He has nothing to offer you except a hard time.

2. The Wimp

Ah, the wimp—he of the gentle manner, artistic sensibilities, kind heart, and poverty-level income. He's the antithesis of all that's macho: The Wimp not only eats quiche, he makes it. But *you'll* have to pay for the ingredients.

Even when the economy's booming, the Wimp doesn't make much money. But you can't hold that against him. What he lacks in funds he makes up for in assets you can't put a price on. He has sensitivity (he cried when he read *The Women's Room*), cultural interests (he likes classical music and modern art), and youthfulness (he's younger than you are, or seems that way).

These are all wonderful qualities, to be sure—when they're hitched to a sense of purpose in life. But the Wimp uses them in lieu of a purpose. He's sensitive, isn't he? Why should he have to achieve? He wants you to carry him, and that's his fatal flaw. His lack of success is excusable, but not his lack of will.

The Wimp's infuriating passivity carries over into bed. Penetration is his downfall. Anyone can be forgiven a few nervous failures at the start, but the Wimp comes back from them only fitfully at best. No matter how splendidly he pleases you through ingenuity or on those special occasions when he slips and connects, sex with a Wimp is never more than marginally satisfying. It's like leading a man around on the dance floor—there's no law against it; it just doesn't feel right.

Don't think a man is a Wimp simply because he earns less than you or might need your financial help. Reserve judgment until you get a picture of his total life situation: Where does he stand as a family man, lover, friend, worker? He's a Wimp only if he's not making it *across the board.* Such wholesale inadequacy may make you want to mother him, but it's a job worse than thankless. It's debilitating. You'll find your inner resources drained by his constant mewling about not getting any "breaks" or not being able to "find" himself. We're all assailed by self-doubts at times, but with the Wimp, they're a way of life.

Betsy, a successful Chicago stockbroker, had a bad experience with a Wimp she took up with when she was feeling desperate for a man. To her friends, clients, and colleagues, Betsy is a remarkable and engaging woman. She's not only talented in her work, but gracious, generous, and strikingly tasteful—the kind of woman who commissions a well-known artist to create poster-size original prints for invitations to her parties.

But with men, Betsy's sensitivity and good taste fail her. Why? For the very reason I touched on earlier—that curious split between competence in work and incompetence in love. As an investment analyst, Betsy had succeeded by softening her aggressiveness to palatable proportions and combining it with an astute sense of what other people wanted and needed. But in love, well—Betsy had been wiped out in an affair fifteen years earlier with a celebrated Washington reporter going through divorce shock. She's still paying for the sin of naïveté, and she wears her excess weight (about thirty pounds) and truculent manner like a linebacker's defense. Half-jokingly, she'll stick out her jaw and demand, "Come on, who'd want a broad like me?"

The answer, of course, is a Wimp. Ken, a muscular, pleasant-faced man of thirty-six, was only a year younger than Betsy but light-years away in getting on in the world. He was a student in the evening-school class Betsy taught in business writing. One night after class, he approached her shyly and showed her a manuscript he was working on—vague, poetic ramblings that had a dreamy quality but no focus. Betsy was noncommittal. Privately, she thought Ken's writing showed no promise—but *he* did.

Over coffee, Betsy learned that Ken had grown up cowed by an abusive father. He was a loner who couldn't seem to get a hold on life. Currently selling waterbeds, he was recovering from a stint as a management trainee with a high-pressure sales organization that turned out to be a cult. Betsy fell in love with him on the spot. She didn't understand that nobody stirs up your nurturing instincts like a Wimp—and leaves your need to be nurtured more unrequited.

Sex with Ken was frustrating. "He managed to perform," Betsy says, "but just barely. Most of the explosive moments were his."

Their relationship went from tenuous to humiliating. Betsy did the courting; Ken was malleable. She didn't mind paying when she took him to her favorite wateringholes like Le Perroquet and the Pump Room (she could write their meals off as a business expense), but she did mind his Wimpish ways. He couldn't conceal his jealousy of Betsy's success, even while enjoying her largesse, and he shamelessly tried to exploit her contacts for himself. "Why the hell can't you make it on your own!" she blurted in a fit of pique after he badgered her once too often for a lead. Ken retaliated sexually. He showed no interest in sex except when he thought Betsy was asleep. Then he'd slip into bed like a thief and tepidly make love to her.

Disgusted, Betsy called it quits. But then she agonized helplessly over Ken for weeks. Relenting, she decided to call him and make amends. That's the sexual hook for you: Having made love to a man, a woman feels that she has to make herself love him—and he may be someone she doesn't even like.

Ken sounded pleased to hear from Betsy, but guarded. When she finally got around to asking him for a date, he told her he was "involved" with someone else. From the way he said it, Betsy knew he was trying to make her jealous. Too annoyed to give him the satisfaction, she wished him well and was starting to say good-bye when Ken suddenly unleashed a torrent of abuse at her. "Goddamn you, you smart-ass dyke!" he screamed. "Why did you call me? I hate ball-breakers like you!"

Betsy hung up on him. She was stunned. Her head reeling, she stared at the phone and silently asked God to strike her dead if she ever so much as looked at another Wimp again.

Luckily, most Wimps are more benign than Ken. You probably won't get anything more scathing from them than some off-the-wall criticism of your work or a string of bitchy little putdowns when they're feeling particularly low. They're a sorrowful lot. But I should tell you that there are some very strong women who actually enjoy and can handle carrying Wimps around on their backs. Unless you fit the description, don't pick one up.

3. The Bleeding Heart

He's suffering from toxic shock over the loss of his wife or girlfriend, and you know it from the way he talks incessantly about her without propriety or pride. His obsession with her has the eerie quality of possession by a demon. You might distract him enough to flirt with you in a woebegone manner, but sleeping with him will be only an act of mercy on your part. He'll perform without even knowing you're there. You're invisible to him—only his pain is real. He's the common variety of the Bleeding Heart.

The less-common variety—the Closet Bleeding Heart—is more dangerous. He's the kind of man who presents himself as "open to new experience," but the experience he's talking about is purely sexual. Only after you yield to him will you discover that he's still bruised and bleeding inside over a broken love affair or marriage and was deceptively using you as a tourniquet for his sorrow.

It's up to you to draw this tricky player out of the closet beforehand and prevent him from exploiting you. Just remember that the Closet Bleeding Heart is also a Lounge Lizard (most of these characters are hybrids rather than purebreds), and you can detect his nefarious motives from his jaded, insincere charm. Our man Warren, again, is an example of this type—a Bleeding Heart trapped inside an exterior of brittle Lizard skin.

I'm particularly fond of Bleeding Hearts—the honest, not the sneaky, ones—because it was just such a man who introduced me to Larry. It happened this way. I was visiting a woman friend who'd invited me to be her guest for cocktails at Elan, the glitzy singles bar in the hotel where she lived. I was having a drink when I bumped into Phil, an amiable fellow I'd gone to high school with and hadn't seen since we both wore braces on our teeth.

Phil was going through an atrocious divorce and had all the earmarks of the full-blown Bleeding Heart—mournful mien, compulsive babbling about his former wife, fixation on the horror. In passing, he mentioned that he knew a wonderful guy for me (Larry) and would give him my number. But the next thing I knew, Phil himself was asking me out—strictly on a platonic basis, of course.

Phil wanted a friend, and I wanted Phil's friend, so we dated a few times. Phil bled, and I mopped patiently. And then came one of those queer turns of events that can be a springboard to an opportunity or land you sprawling in a trap. Phil asked me out for New Year's Eve. He lived in the same town as Larry, an hour and a half away, and he wanted me to come down a day ahead of time and stay at his home. His plan was that Larry would drop in to meet me while I was Phil's house-guest. I was certain Phil's motives were pure, but I was too seasoned a player to take unnecessary chances. I declined.

Soon after, Larry called and asked me out (in the revolving door in your life, one man's exit is another man's entrance). Larry not only made a date but agreed to pick me up on my home turf, the ideal place for best impressions.

I give you this as an object lesson on how to handle the garden-variety Bleeding Heart: Be kind to him. Befriend him. But let him know, unmistakably, that you're looking for someone whose heart has healed.

4. El Cheapo

If you're lucky, he'll spring for dinner at a medium-priced restaurant on your first date, and might even throw in a carafe of wine to go with the meal. But this treat is only a "loss leader"—he's using this display of extravagance as an inducement to do business. Don't expect to see the likes of it again. From there on in, it's pasta at his place. If you ever get inside a restaurant a second time with El Cheapo, be prepared to do one of three things: Pick up the check; "contribute" (pay half); or "share" (he buys one meal and orders an extra plate for you).

I'm not suggesting that a man has to take you out in high style all the time to demonstrate genuine caring, or that you shouldn't pay your way as you see fit. Giving a man a cut rate on a relationship is warranted if he can show good cause and a generally appealing character. But El Cheapo can't. His miserliness, unlike the Wimp's, exists independently of his earnings. El Cheapo is stingy whether he has money or not. He's stingy with himself—and there's the rub: *He can't share.*

One El Cheapo I know has a lucrative law practice and supports himself handsomely on it—but *only* himself. He'll go on trips to Tibet to indulge his passion for archaeology, but he won't take you around the corner to the deli for a sandwich. He specializes in free concerts (*he* has a season ticket to the Met) or amateur theatricals (*he* hasn't missed a Tony winner yet by himself), followed by free sex at your place (pound for pound, that's the best entertainment value around). Forget that he won't spend money—he won't spend the *night* at your place, but insists on going back to his cave to spend the night alone.

Since that first "loss leader" might fool you, be on the lookout for these clues that the man who's making a grandstand play for you could be El Cheapo:

• He depends on low-priced singles functions as his main source of social contacts. You won't find him in the better bars and lounges, and that's a plus for them—they draw mostly bad risks, but they're not *stingy* bad risks.

• He has a solitary life-style and inordinate need for privacy which he might try to conceal from you. A middle-aged, never-married El Cheapo, for example, is not above lying about a brief early marriage but won't give details about this "youthful mistake" (a code phrase favored by confirmed bachelors to avoid scaring women off).

• He exhibits a forbidding expertise about discounts, bargains, and cost-cutting. You have a vision of him walking through a relationship with a pocket calculator.

No man, before he's made a commitment, can be expected to spend money on you as liberally as he might afterward. Temporary flashes of stinginess in a date who's basically generous can be construed as ordinary prudence. But there's nothing ordinary about El Cheapo's prudence—it's carried to infinity.

5. The Couch Case

Now we come to the grab bag of assorted weirdos, wackos, space cadets, neurotics, and psychotics who appeal to women because they're "challenging." But the challenges they present can't be met except by a professional therapist, and even that's doubtful, considering the monumental resistance of most of these Couch Cases, hereinafter referred to as "Couchies."

These are men who are too far gone in their abnormality to be helped. They don't want to be helped—they want to be humored. Couchies have no use for you if you won't go along with their craziness. From their warped perspective of the world, they're right—it's everyone else who should be in treatment.

A Couchie draws you in through the power of the unpredictable. He's exciting because you never know what to expect. One minute he's more kind and loving than anyone you've ever known; the next he's more hateful. He binds you to him by working your anxieties. He makes other men seem boring in comparison because they're consistent. And that's why the Couchie is a trap: You can't love a man divided against himself without falling into the breach. His ambivalence is like quicksand—the more you try to accommodate him, the deeper you sink.

Many Couchies are exceptionally bright professionals who are earning a high income and enjoying a luxurious life-style.

They've succeeded in spite of themselves, and you might be tempted to overlook aberrations in a nutty doctor or lawyer that you'd never tolerate in someone less accomplished. But don't be distracted by status and illusions of the good life. An overachieving Couchie is still "half a loaf"—and a nonnegotiable half, at that. How can you hope to make a go of it when the defective half is something so vital as the other person's mental health?

I don't mean to be cynical or callous about this. To be human is to be compassionate toward our own and others' imperfections. But when we meet a deeply disturbed man, one who still seems very desirable, it's a trap to think that we can kiss his emotional wounds and make them better. It takes a healthy respect for our own limitations to admit that a Couchie is beyond our scope. That's what shrinks are for, and many of them are seeing women who might not be there if the men they'd gotten involved with had been induced to go.

Whatever the particular nature of a Couchie's disturbance, it precludes a viable long-term relationship with him because he won't let you live your own life. He'll exhibit signs of this rigidity early on, and if you know what's good for you, you'll run for the nearest exit as soon as you see them.

Marlene, a tall, sexy-looking manager of her own employment agency, rues the day that one of her clients fixed her up with an architect whom she now affectionately refers to as "Son of Sam." By their second date, Marlene knew there was something wrong with Sam, but she was already sexually hooked and running scared (her parents had died recently and she'd separated from her husband).

They were going to the beach that day, and Sam insisted on making the bed first. Nothing wrong with that, except that he covered the bedspread with a sheet to keep it from getting soiled while they were gone. Then he took a book to read and wrapped it in aluminum foil so it wouldn't get discolored by the sun. He washed the car—twice—and they were off.

Lured by the "challenge" of bringing around a Couchie who had money and social position, Marlene good-naturedly put up with Sam's bizarre obsessions. He responded by becoming a dictator with Marlene, intent on controlling every aspect of her life. He screamed at her and smacked her around for the least infraction of his rules, and then won her back by being very contrite, generous, and tender. Their relationship turned incredibly mean and ugly, but Sam had Marlene convinced that she'd be crazy to leave him. It took a psychiatrist to convince Marlene that she'd be crazy to stay.

My friend Wendy's experience with a Couchie was the worst atrocity of her single days, and it never would have happened if she hadn't started running scared after the sudden breakup of a yearlong relationship. Yielding to hysteria, Wendy picked up the phone and called a divorced doctor whose name she spotted in her address book. He'd been a childhood friend and sometime date. Two years earlier, when he'd returned from Marin County, California (the natural habitat of the Couchie), to reestablish his practice in the East, he'd looked Wendy up and badgered her into going out with him. He was brilliant and cultured but much too weird for her and she soon tired of the relationship.

Wendy still remembers his rage at the world; he was always railing obnoxiously at waitresses, tradespeople, drivers on the road—while she cringed in embarrassment. He was an only child who couldn't forgive the world for having other people in it. His inconsideration knew no bounds: He would wait until Wendy had dinner on the table, then bolt into another room and kneel on the floor for twenty minutes, doing TM.

Desperation breeds forgiveness. Wendy blotted out his eccentricities and forced herself to recall how romantic and affectionate he'd been. It didn't occur to her that the balance of power had changed. He had been chasing her before, and she'd had the upper hand. She had no idea what she was in for now that she was on the run.

On their first date, Wendy sat by herself in a high-school auditorium and applauded dutifully while he performed a minor role in a little theater-group production of *Damn Yankees*. Afterward, he took her to a cast party at somebody's home where the big excitement of the evening was watching a blurry videotape of the previous cast party. Wendy should have quit then and there, but she made her own pact with the devil to continue the relationship rather than be alone. That's when she learned that a bad relationship only gets worse the second time around.

Dr. Couch Case still ranted and raved at everyone, but now he was abusive and overbearing with Wendy, too. He broke dates at the last minute and hung up the phone on her when he didn't like what she said. He called her at all hours of the day and night and yelled at her children for not telling him where she was. He ran her ragged helping him out when his secretary quit (who could work for him?), and then became infuriated because Wendy wouldn't get out of bed at three o'clock in the morning to perform road service when he totaled his car driving home from the hospital. To punish her for this insubordination, he scratched her from his summer vacation plans and took her rival, a widow, away to his cottage in Long Beach Island.

After he came back, he showed up at Wendy's house unexpectedly in his new fire-engine-red MG, tooting the horn like a kid. That weekend, he abducted her early Saturday morning and made her accompany him on a whirlwind tour. First they went to the widow's apartment in downtown Philadelphia to pick up his clothes (they'd had a fight); then on to his opera lesson; from there to a marina in Delaware to buy a boat. They ended up in a roadside inn near Baltimore; he picked a place where he could join a musician he knew at the piano bar while Wendy sat at the dinner table by herself and applauded dutifully. She had a feeling of déjà vu.

The end of the relationship was as churlish and explosive

as Dr. Couch Case himself. He knew Wendy had begun dating someone else, and that made him uneasy enough to condescend to pick her up at the airport when she came back from a business trip in Detroit. Knowing how unreliable he was, she had misgivings, but it was such a novel idea that he should do something for her for a change that she accepted.

Miraculously, he was on time. He insisted that he cook dinner for Wendy that night and, in his maniacal fashion, whisked her away to his condo.

It would have been a lovely dinner except that Wendy received a telephone call midway through the meal. It was from the young woman who was Wendy's administrative assistant in her company. Wendy asked her to call back, but she said she was leaving the office and would take only a minute to go over an important matter. She began briefing Wendy as quickly as possible when Dr. Couch Case, who was annoyed that Wendy was taking a business call on his time, told her very curtly, "Why don't you take that in the other room."

Wendy could hear him sullenly chomping on his steak while she finished her call in the study. By the time she got back to the table, he was already in the kitchen, clearing his plate. Then he got a call. He made it obvious that the caller was the widow of the Long Beach Island caper, and he embarked on an extended conversation with her for Wendy's benefit.

Furious, Wendy left the room. When he came after her some time later, she thanked him for dinner and politely asked if he would take her home. He flew into a rage. He couldn't see that he'd hurt her, only that she was committing the unpardonable sin of rejecting him. He called her "a neurotic bitch" and told her she would end up "a lonely, bitter old woman."

While they screamed at each other at the top of their lungs, he called a cab. He wanted Wendy to wait outside in a torrential downpour, but she stood her ground. When the cab came, she strode past him without so much as a backward glance. The epilogue to the story is that Wendy is now happily married, and Dr. Couch Case is still miserably alone.

How can you tell if a man is a lovable oddball, strange but harmless, or an unlovable Couchie? A Couchie is different from all other men because he has abandoned the decency—the "human impulse," as it's called—that's the barest minimum needed for love. When he loses control, he'll do the forbidden—punch a woman with his fists, throw her out nude in the snow, destroy her possessions. He lacks the sense of limits that other people have.

Because a Couchie will stop at nothing, you can never do enough for him. His love isn't nourishing; it consumes. A continuing relationship with him is bound to fail, and you'll come away from it riddled with self-doubt because a Couchie needs to project his worst fears about himself—that he's sick, selfish, unlovable—onto you.

Like the little girl with the curl in the middle of her forehead, a Couchie can be irresistibly appealing when he's under control. But sooner or later, unless you have a rare talent for masochism, he'll become unbearable.

Just remember this: Your first loss with a Couchie is your best and cheapest loss. Don't go back.

If you can possibly help it, don't go at all.

6. *Somebody's Husband*

Unless there are extraordinary extenuating circumstances, comparable to those that justify euthanasia, for example, I'm opposed on moral grounds to infidelity.

It also runs counter to my philosophy of lovemanship—that a woman does best in love by learning how to exert her own power effectively. That's very difficult to do when there's an unknown imbalance of power built into the equation by the man's wife. How great or how little that imbalance is depends on a number of factors: the tenor of the marital relationship, the presence and ages of children, the man's financial resources, what divorce means to him.

It's impossible to say that Somebody's Husband is always a trap, because there are many women—and their numbers seem to be growing—who have pulled off a viable relationship with one. But it's not an easy feat. It almost makes discipline and bondage with a single man look good in comparison: The punishment is more imaginative, and he's available full-time.

A woman can win with Somebody's Husband only by working around the degrading circumstances imposed by the nature of the game to build a relationship so compelling that the man must have it at all costs. The sexual hook is often her greatest strength, but it'll be useless if she isn't the right woman for the job—right for his personality, his social circle, his children, his relatives, whatever's important to him. If she isn't, no matter how good sex is, he's not going to make her Somebody's Next Wife.

More often than not, Somebody's Husband *is* a trap because there isn't a woman living who can induce him to get out of his marriage. He wants you *in addition to*, not *in place of*, and nothing you can do will change that. He's a trap because he may make single men, who don't have the benefit of a wife, look doubtful and insecure. But accessible men are the real opportunities. Somebody's Husband may pretend to want the best for you, but secretly he enjoys deflecting you away from your better options and throwing your mind into confusion over them. What does *he* have to lose? From his position of safety, he's not playing the game—he's playing with *you*.

Snapping Your Losing Streak

I haven't pointed out these traps to you to deter you from ever taking a risk in love or opening yourself to vulnerability. I just want to impress upon you that there are times when losing is a foregone conclusion. You can learn from your losses, but there's a point of no return. When you lose badly enough or too consistently through your own recklessness, that's when you become afraid to risk or be vulnerable when you should.

I can assure you that the opportunities are out there, and there are more of them than you think. The worst is a product of your own "last chance" mentality: You've conditioned yourself to think that you have to take what you find; and since you're not looking intelligently, what you're finding is the tip of the iceberg. The men you're meeting in your grab-bag fashion are like the jobs in the "Help Wanted" ads—they're only the most *visible* part of the action, and usually not the best.

You won't find the opportunities (and they won't find you) until you change your "last chance" attitude. Understand that you're going after a rewarding relationship—not a commitment, necessarily—that can't happen while you're spinning your wheels in the traps because you're lazy, afraid of failure, or afraid of success. I've been all three at different times in my life, and I know how they can inhibit you. Sometimes you're lazy about men because your work or your children come first, and that's a positive choice that may outlive its usefulness. As for the fear of failure or its close relative, the fear of success (if I get this man, what'll I *do* with him?), no one is entirely free of these two deadweights, but you have to get out on the track in spite of them if you want to win.

Motivation is the beginning of change. Think of the rewards that await you when you're in control of your choices in love—companionship, affection, empathy, sharing, loyalty, and sex that's so good it's extraterrestrial—and *shape up!* Kiss the traps good-bye. It's time to take leave of the first phase of your education in love.

MORAL: Instant love vanishes instantly.

COROLLARIES:

Rule 1. You can't start off with the end result (relationships are built, not found).

Rule 2. Your chances are only as good as your choices (you can't blame him for turning out to be what you knew he was when you met him).

4

How to Manage Dating and Earn Experience Points

*I*n Dungeons and Dragons, a fantasy adventure game for children and bright adults, the players assume the roles of mythical characters who gain experience by overcoming perils and winning treasures. Each session of the game is an exciting adventure created by the Dungeon Master to test the characters' abilities—strength, intelligence, wisdom, dexterity, constitution, and charisma—by pitting them against "magic-user spells," "character attacks," encounters with "undead monsters," and other fantastic obstacles. As the characters survive these adventures and pile up experience points (or XP), they grow in power and ability.

Why am I telling you all this? Because I think Dungeons and Dragons is a great metaphor for the love game. The Dungeon Master is like the fortunes of romance, and the magic spells and monsters are the difficulties most of us have to overcome in the struggle to find lasting love.

Dungeons and Dragons is similar to the love game because "winning" and "losing" are not the same as they are in other games. As the "Basic Rulebook" says, "Everyone is here to have fun." The Dungeon Master doesn't play against the players or take sides, but simply tries to move the game along with humor as well as excitement. Winning treasure (a man) doesn't end the game, nor is the game lost when an unlucky player's character dies (he stops calling). The player may simply "roll up" a new character and continue playing.

So it is with relationships. You're not dead when one ends, and dating becomes a continuously unfolding adventure after you summon the courage to play the game step by step instead of trying to bribe fate and win all at once. Success doesn't happen overnight anywhere, which explains why get-love-quick schemes are mostly futile and why dating a variety of men for experience points is preferable to latching on to the nearest one for a quick commitment.

The dating adventure helps you learn how to function when it's not a monogamous situation—a basic skill that can save you from ending up alone or getting stuck in a rotten relationship because you can't handle the stress of being unattached. Dating also teaches you what men find magical or disenchanting about you and what you find magical or disenchanting in a man. The more specific you can become about these things, the more you'll cut down your margin for error in the future and sharpen your sense of direction. Don't resent the hassle and the "wasted" time—dating is your chance to have fun while learning on the job.

Finding *dates*, as opposed to stumbling upon traps, is a consequence of setting up enough time in your life to do what you have to do and be where you have to be to make yourself known to the right people. Men who want more than a transient, casual relationship (or people who know these men and might refer them to you) are out there like an untapped market that has to be reached. Connecting with them is a matter of cause and effect. You've got to put together a salable product and promote it like crazy in the social circles you move in or would like to enter, and then skillfully take advantage of the results. In effect, your social life is another vocation, and the rewards will be commensurate with how well you master the challenges it presents.

Social Security at Any Age

It may not hit you during the week, but on Saturday night the absence of a social life comes at you with the force of a torpedo. Suddenly you're drowning in time, a Black Sea of empty hours. I don't care what you've heard about "creative loneliness," most of us don't have the capacity to sit at home on a Saturday night in solitary, four-wall confinement and get a high from thinking deep thoughts. The deepest thought we keep thinking under such circumstance is *When will it be Monday?*

Men haven't been culturally trained to believe they're nothing without a woman, and yet many of them are as vulnerable to "Saturday-night fever" as we are. They're no less mortified if they have to spend a weekend alone. The prospect of spending countless weekends alone so unnerves men who've been married that 80 percent of them remarry within two years of divorce (compared to our 75 percent within four years). Men clearly don't like living without us any more than we like living without them, only they're better equipped to do something about it. They get all the numbers to call, while we usually wait for our number to come up.

That's the "undead monster" we have to slay—this *lack of control* over our own social contacts—not our need for a man. The women I know who tried to talk themselves out of wanting an intimate relationship only confused themselves and wasted their mental breath. Wanting an attachment is not some ridiculous relic from our prom-queen days; it's as legitimate as the need for food and shelter. The person who is as happy as a clam living alone has either made a heroic adaptation or is lying.

No less an authority than "the father of loneliness research," sociologist Robert Weiss, has identified a sense of attachment through an intimate relationship as one of two social conditions human beings need in order not to feel lonely. The other is a sense of community, of belonging to a group, through a network of friends who share our interests and concerns.

During my single days I made an interesting discovery about attachments and community: Your worst attachments are made when you're isolated, and your best attachments materialize when your social network is radiating in all directions.

Networks operate on the "magnetic field" principle. Their purpose is to help you enjoy life *without* a man, but they inadvertently draw men to you like a magnet. Once you realize that picking up men is not the answer to loneliness, you start picking up friends, who in turn get you involved in activities that are pleasurable and enriching in themselves but also result in the best contacts. And the three most important ways to meet eligible men are contacts, contacts, contacts. As your network grows, so will your volume of dates.

A network becomes even more valuable to you *after* the dates have arrived. The social security provided by having people other than dates to go out with—women friends, married couples, your children, groups or organizations—is what enables you to relax on a date and perform more capably. When you're not depending on *this one man* for companionship, you're less likely to overplay your hand and frighten him away with your intensity. Women who are driven to ask "When am I going to see you again?" usually don't.

A woman who's socially active holds a dual fascination for a man. She's intrinsically interesting because she's constantly expanding the scope of her knowledge and experience—doing things, going places, meeting people. And she's extrinsically interesting because her repertoire of people, places, and things excites a man's curiosity: If he's not taking her to the latest hit movie or concert, who is?

You don't have to localize your network; let it spread from coast to coast. In today's age of mobility, the "geographically undesirable" person has been phased out of existence (the G.U.

never really existed at all except as a fiction in lazy minds). Several couples I know are happily married or living together after long-distance commuting courtships (New York to San Diego; Detroit to Hartford; Philadelphia to Miami) that were promoted by network intermediaries.

The only way to build a social network is to *organize* your free time instead of letting it sneak up on you from behind. The solitary life can be habit-forming because it spares you planning, effort, and expense. But that empty weekend rolls around with loathsome regularity if you don't fill it beforehand.

In my single days (before I saw the light), when I didn't have a relationship going, I thought I could dodge responsibility for my social life by burying myself in my work. I pulled it off during the week, but the weekends refused to be tricked. Try as I would to concentrate on paper work I'd brought home from the office or a manuscript in progress, I couldn't get a thing done. I was always assailed by a feeling that I was dreadfully out of step with the rest of the population, and I wound up not only idle but depressed.

Deliverance came from a woman friend who indoctrinated me almost against my will into networking. Vivian had an approach to the singles world that reminded me of the "buddy system" at summer camp: Always travel in twos. Before I met her, I thought there was something shameful about being publicly "single," but Vivian forced me out of the closet. She insisted that we go clubbing, dragged me to singles dances, and even got me a date with the friend of a man she was seeing (that's *teamwork*). I reciprocated by bolstering her spirits through trying times, and our friendship opened up a rewarding chain of contacts. It was Vivian I'd gone to see in her new apartment when I bumped into Phil, the man who introduced me to Larry.

Whether your social network leads you to a man or not is immaterial. Attend to it lovingly. Make regular dates *in advance* with friends (of either sex) to go to dinner, movies, shows, concerts, museums, lectures, meetings, ball games, vacation spots. Your network may not be a substitute for an intimate relationship, but it puts the *living* into living alone. Desperation has no greater enemy—and you no greater friend—than richly booked time.

Your Personal Package

The newest gurus in the business world are the "personal-image consultants"—those packaging experts who, for a hefty fee, will help you get ahead on the job by telling you what to do about your wardrobe, hairstyle, cosmetics, speech, and posture. The theory behind such personal packaging is that the right look is a self-fulfilling prophecy. If you change your appearance to reflect poise, confidence, and success, the experts say, you'll *feel* and *act* poised, confident, and successful, and others will react to you accordingly.

Big-league corporations like Gulf Oil and General Motors routinely pay image-makers $10,000 per group seminar, and growing numbers of ambitious individuals are spending upwards of $1,000 a day to get "the look." Books like John Molloy's *Dress for Success* are still flying off the shelves. Executives are hearing from Harvard that the "corporate culture," which includes styles of dress, is more important than the bottom line. What does all this tell us? That the psychology of appearance is no lie.

For years I was one of those women who had no use for the dictates of fashion. To me, elegance was remembering to take the dry cleaner's tag off my skirt before wearing it. I was careless about my weight and privately regarded clothes-conscious women as wimps who were kowtowing to male standards of taste. My thinking was distorted by a common confusion about substance and style: I thought that because substance was more important, it made style unnecessary.

It was only periodically, when I had to go on promotional

tours, that I acknowledged the impact of image and whipped myself into shape. Before my fourth tour in the spring of 1980, I shed twenty-eight pounds in ten weeks! Concomitantly, my dates with men increased in inverse proportion to my weight: The less I weighed, the more dates I had.

On the advice of an unofficial image-maker (one of my dates), I got a chic hairdo, had my ears pierced, and bought some glamorous clothes in preparation for my appearances on TV. Again, my luck with men improved astonishingly. I went on the road imbued with a new respect for the advice in the cigarette ad: "A Woman Should Be Both Thin and Rich."

Looking rich doesn't necessarily mean springing for expensive clothes that defy your means or personal preferences in fashion. Rich is a matter of taste, not price. There's plenty of latitude between a Lizard's morbid preoccupation with trendiness and a wholesome regard for what sets you off to good advantage. I still think that being too well coordinated (the plastic mannequin look) is off-putting to men. The ideal seems to be thin and rich but also vulnerable.

If you don't have a savvy friend who can help you out, it might pay to invest in an hour's consultation with a fashion expert (some affordable ones advertise in the classified section of the leading women's magazines). Without making a fetish of it, practice the psychology of appearance. There are countless people who suddenly found their objectives in love much easier to attain when they did nothing more substantive than make a few outward improvements.

Concern with personal packaging in romance is not wimpish in women—it's good business. Whether you like it or not, everyone perceives and judges you within thirty seconds of the first eye contact. Much of what we think of as spontaneous sexual "chemistry" is the projection of attractive qualities through carefully cultivated image. When you invest in making your first impression as engaging as possible, you're actually buying time to reinforce the message that there *is* substance—intelligence, warmth, humor, vitality—beneath that winsome style.

If anything, attention to image is more critical in your personal life than it is in business, because it goes beyond first
impressions to the heart of women's desperation about men.
When you start giving yourself the life-style to which you'd
like to become accustomed—fixing up your surroundings, buying yourself "toys"—looking for a man is not such a desperate
search for a sponsor anymore. (You can achieve the same effect
by adjusting your image *downward*, if necessary—do you really
need a pedicure every three days?—so that you're living within
your means and not casting about frantically for a man to
provide deficit funding.) To paraphrase Gloria Steinem's quip,
most of us should become the husband we want to marry.

Like being your own best friend, becoming your own husband is a hard idea to put into practice. I didn't get the hang
of it until I was old enough to be my *second* husband. On my
forty-seventh birthday, I made my ultimate connubial gesture
as a single woman: I took $5,000 of my savings and bought
myself a Black Diamond mink coat. I didn't think I could afford
it any more than the woman who's chewing her fingernails
worrying about next month's rent. My cash reserve wasn't the
problem; getting up the nerve to spend it on myself was. Next
to paying a man alimony, buying yourself a mink coat may be
the most audacious act of financial independence a woman is
capable of.

You don't have to spend $5,000 to buy yourself parity with
men in the love game. Any amount will do. Whatever con-
stitutes being "rich" for you at this stage of your life—invest
in it. Don't be a lady-in-waiting, postponing the good life until
you meet a man who'll subsidize it for you. Become your own
husband, and your fear of never finding one will loosen its iron
grip. Your performance anxiety on dates will diminish, and
your options multiply. What's more, your relatively elegant
life-style will signal to a man who's afraid of getting financially
ripped off in a relationship (they all are), "Hey, I'm capable

of doing my share." Living well, you see, is not only the best revenge, it's a compelling stroke of personal power.

A Live One

You've done all your steps—built your network, made your contacts, glossed your image—and suddenly there's a live one on the line. He got your number from his cousin Barbara, who's taking the dream-analysis class you signed up for with a friend you met at an antinuke rally you went to because one of your tennis buddies talked you into it.

He's impressive on the phone, and you make a date. In person, he turns out to be presentable, intelligent, friendly, sincere, capable, generous, and reasonably sane (God bless Cousin Barbara—and Freud, for inventing dream analysis). It's too early to tell how well you'll connect in a serious relationship, but you know you're staring a bona-fide opportunity in the eye. Where do you go from here?

You put your best foot forward—*one step at a time.* You do *not* crowd him. You do *not* engage in overkill. You're trying to earn experience points (XP), remember? Using high-pressure tactics to lock up a quick commitment will work against you. You'll either abort a budding relationship before its time or, if successful, force a commitment from someone who might be a good opportunity temporarily (an interim job) but a dead end in the long run.

Karen, an aggressive real-estate agent, got carried away with closing deals in her private life. By the time she was forty, she'd been through three grueling divorces because she felt compelled to marry all of her "involvements." Now she's dating an obvious "temporary" who takes her out in high style and also to bed, but she cheerfully acknowledges that she doesn't want him as a permanent partner and has no intention of marrying him. Meantime, she's not sitting on the sidelines.

She's out there developing her lovemanship skills and having a good time.

The nature of romance today—sex before love—makes it almost mandatory for you to learn how to enjoy an *uncommitted* sexual relationship without feeling obliged to justify it with a commitment. A dating relationship will rise or fall on its own merits. If you can allow it a life of its own and be prepared to take your earned XP as your only prize, you'll have mastered the most important part of your basic training for eventual success in love. Nothing will stand you in better stead than the ability to let a relationship evolve until you know that it's *this man* you want, and not a commitment as its own reward.

5

Keeping a Live One Alive

*A*relationship with a live one is like a finicky houseplant—it'll stay alive much longer if you don't overfeed it. Given the right environment, it might even blossom into a beautiful commitment. But the more powerless you are in the face of your commitment mania, the less likely are the chances of that happening. So here are a handful of hints to help you grow in power through the dating adventure.

1. Nobody Loves a Bloodhound

Many a live one has been turned into a fugitive by a woman's dogged persistence in the early stages of a relationship. Desire vanishes quickly under duress. No one, not even a customer in a department store, likes to be badgered into a choice or hounded to make up his mind before he's ready. A good persuader must have the patience and sensitive self-control not to *overreach*—to slip from trying into overtrying—and not to use the kind of force that sets up resistance.

Women have to be the hidden persuaders in most relationships because men see more danger in intimacy than women do. (Women, according to Harvard psychologist Carol Gilligan, see more danger arising from competitive achievement than from intimacy, and are more likely than men to associate danger with isolation.) When a woman meets a good candidate for a relationship, her natural tendency is to move quickly toward a serious involvement; his natural tendency is to proceed with caution. The woman, therefore, must discipline herself to make haste more slowly than she would if left to her own devices.

One of the hardest tests you'll have to face is the battle with Ma Bell—resisting the impulse to call him more than you should. Let's say you've been out with him a couple of times and you're waiting for him to call you to make the next date. You're trying to read the new Ludlum thriller, but your mind is tortured with thoughts of him: *What's he doing now? Who's he with?* You glance at the phone. It refuses to ring. It mocks you with its implacable silence. You turn away and resume reading, determined to give him a little more time to call you—a few hours, another day. But you're no match for Ma Bell. The phone begins to exert a strange hold over you, slowly pulling you toward it. Unable to stop yourself, you put down your book and reach for the receiver.

If you're lucky, he won't be home. Fate will have intervened and done for you what you couldn't do yourself—*respect his right to go at his own pace.*

While you're trying to launch a relationship, you should never let impatience or fear drive you to do anything that might make him feel under the gun. I'm reminded here of a scene from *Absence of Malice*, the movie about a newspaper reporter (Sally Field) who sets up the guiltless and gorgeous forty-five-year-old owner of a distillery (Paul Newman) as the subject of one of her exposés. Besides getting him into trouble, she also tries to get him into bed. When he seems taken aback by her blunt overture, she quickly explains: "I'm thirty-four. I don't need courting." And he comes back with "I'm from the Stone Age—I *do*. I'd like to think it was my idea."

Whether he's from the Stone Age or the age of punk rock, he's going to want to think it's at least *half* his idea—and he's entitled to that. After all, isn't equality of the sexes our ideal? Strive for equality at the outset. If you want a *live* one and not a stuffed trophy to display to your family and friends, don't try to drag an indifferent man into a relationship by his heels. Brute strength is a mask for raw dependency, which is something you must learn to control if you want to develop the skills and power for genuine love.

When bloodhound tactics backfire, as they usually do, you find that the damage to your dignity is worse than the loss of the man. Jackie, a feisty little graphic artist in her mid-twenties, began dating Steve when she was desperate to get out of a bad relationship (some relationships create more desperation than they relieve). Steve showed interest in Jackie until she started pounding after him relentlessly. "He liked me," says Jackie, "but he wasn't ready to have someone call him every day and send him romantic greeting cards and cute little presents."

As Jackie's campaign intensified, Steve's interest evaporated—"He just stopped calling," she says. Beside herself, Jackie lost that last shred of pride that keeps a pursuer from becoming a pest. "It galled me that he was dating other women," she admits, "so I started trailing him around and creating tacky scenes." After it was over, Jackie realized that it wasn't love that had made a fool of her, but her obsession with winning through intimidation.

I'm not saying that you can't nail a man with such coercive tactics as "love-bombing" and playing on his guilt, but a commitment like that is rarely worth the blood it's written in. Men who've been cornered into a commitment tend to cheat, become workaholics, or distance themselves emotionally in other ways because they feel bored or suffocated.

You can improve your dating performance, and possibly spare yourself a bad case of addictive love somewhere down the line, by keeping your bloodhound tendencies on a tight leash.

Don't make that call! When you feel the urge to call him and you know you shouldn't, call a friend instead (that's what networks are for). If your friend isn't home, stuff the telephone cord in your mouth and do a primal scream until the urge passes. And buy yourself an answering machine, if you're attempting to live alone without one, so that you don't have to sit in homebound agony waiting for his calls. Now's the time to get out and about as much as possible and to involve yourself in projects that will keep your mind from dwelling on what he's doing when he's not calling you.

Not hearing from him for a week or two doesn't necessarily mean the worst. He could be up to his hairline in work or family matters or meetings of the Trout-Fishing Society (it doesn't *always* have to be another woman). But a man who's been busy for a month, even innocently, may find it awkward to call. A friendly follow-up call from you after a week of biting the cord, or a pleasant note in the mail, could be timely.

What if he has indeed met someone else and is preoccupied with her? Be thankful for early losses—they're easier to absorb than later ones. Rise to the challenge and be gracious to him. You don't know that he won't be back (some men go through the revolving door in your life more than once) or that he won't become an advocate of yours in the future with other men. Take the long-range view: A date is only one night, but a contact is forever.

2. *Too Much Too Soon*

He calls you up at midnight because he's dying for a late-night pizza; and you, craving only a good night's sleep, drag yourself out of bed to accommodate him. He shows up in an old coat with a button that's starting to come off, and you whip out a needle and thread and attend to it on the spot. He mentions in passing that he's having car trouble, and the next day you let your work slide while you spend an hour on the phone, lining up six estimates for transmission repairs.

Traditional subservience may get you your man—but then what? After months (or years) of being constantly available to him and anticipating his every need, the die is cast. You've created your own job description, and you're stuck with it. The first time you try to beg off because you're tired or you have your own work to do or you've made other plans— perfectly legitimate reasons—he's going to cry "Foul!" (or other epithets you'll like even less).

Paula, a divorced schoolteacher, spent seven months "getting" Jeff by being the earth mother of his dreams. She asked not what he could do for her, but only what she could do for him—and he told her. They never went out to dinner on dates because Jeff hated restaurants (Paula loved them). Paula did all of the driving because Jeff was tired from the stress of his job (so was Paula, who had a family to take care of after she came home from work). Paula skipped dental and medical appointments so she could run errands for Jeff (he jogged in his free time, and Paula developed infections).

"He was testing me," Paula explains, "and I wanted to gain his trust. I thought I should make myself indispensable to him first, and assert myself later."

But Paula found that she'd painted herself into a corner. After Jeff began living with her, paying most of her bills and improving her life-style, her attempts to modify her geisha-girl routine provoked his wrath. He accused her of trying to take him over, and they engaged in heated battles with increasing bitterness on both sides. They finally broke up, each blaming the other for the failure of the relationship.

Paula's method of investing in love—pay more than you can afford up front, and adjust the price downward after you make a deal—is based on the old belief in women's powerlessness with men. The idea is that you have no power in the relationship until the man gives it to you through a commitment.

But by then, it's often too late. If you haven't locked yourself into an untenable position, like Paula, you may be burned out from expending all that "sweat equity" (labor offered as part of the purchase price). Now, when you have the commitment you've always wanted, you're too resentful and depleted to make it work.

In contrast to women, men have a much more sensible, if infuriating, method of investing in a relationship. They're not given to impulse buying. Men who've been trained to compete in the business world are wary of plunking everything they own into a situation before thoroughly testing it out. In the testing period, they limit their investment to what they think they can safely afford. They hold back on exhaustive "sweat equity" (and diamonds) until they're convinced that they've found someone who warrants a full-scale commitment. Unlike put-upon women who feel they must retrench after they "have" a man, most men become more giving and generous once a commitment is made.

Men are encouraged by the culture to be more assertive than women, and that accounts for this difference. Personally, I think men have the right idea. A desirable man doesn't over-extend himself in love to the point where winning becomes a hollow victory. He sets the tone early on by letting a woman know that while she's important to him, even paramount to him, he's not going to re-create himself in her image to get her.

Not giving too much too soon in a relationship is a test of your power to take the preferred risk. It's better to risk losing a man by setting limits on what you can do for him than to risk creating the monster of an impossible role. No one—and that includes your mother, your boss, and your best girl-friend—will show respect for your own time, plans, energy, and needs if you don't. Your double flips and handsprings may not even be appealing to a man you're trying to please if he thinks they convey a lack of self-respect or a grand design to get him first and redo him later.

3. The Star Syndrome

A New York bachelor I know had a brief affair with a rising star in the business world who liked him but didn't have the time. When he tired of talking to her Phone-Mate, he called her at her office during working hours to make a date. Here, as he tells it, is what that dialogue was like.

SHE: (*Briskly*) Hello.
(*The telephone speaker makes her voice sound distant as it broadcasts their conversation throughout the office.*)

HE: (*Cheerfully*) Hello, Sue? This is Hank. I hope I haven't caught you at a—

SHE: Don't be silly, Hank. It's good to hear from you. Say, can you hold on a minute? (*He gets an earful of silence while she takes another call. Then she comes back on, all creamy smoothness and efficiency.*) Sorry about that, Hank. How've you been?

HE: Oh, fine, Sue. Listen, I was wondering if you'd like to go to the Rolling Stones concert on—

SHE: (*Calling out sharply*) Estelle, don't put that in the out basket yet—I'm not finished with it! (*More calmly*) Yes, Hank. You were saying something about the Rolling Stones?

HE: Yeah, I've got tickets for Saturday, the nineteenth. Would you like to go?

SHE: (*Rustling papers impatiently*) Terry, where's the budget narrative on direct and indirect costs? (*Apologetically*) I'm afraid I can't make it on the nineteenth, Hank. I'll be at a management seminar in Scottsdale, Arizona. Can we make it another time?

HE: Well, what about dinner Friday night, the eighteenth?

SHE: I'd love to, but that's my racketball night.

HE: (*Jokingly*) What about a year from next Wednesday?

SHE: (*Flipping her desk calendar*) Nope, I'm having dinner with a client.

HE: (*Crestfallen*) Well, I guess that's about it, then.

SHE: (*Impassively*) Thanks for calling, Hank. Take care.

The New Woman complains that men are intimidated by her success, competence, and intelligence, when in fact it's her *self-importance* that repels men in droves. She's too busy being busy. Accomplishment is attractive—the conspicuous display of it isn't.

You may be using your achievements as a stick to hold men at bay or to bludgeon them over the head without even being aware of it. As impressive as your new authority may be to you, to men it speaks of frightening female inroads on their turf.

Try to display your success with sensitivity if you don't want it to overwhelm a man or incur his resentment. But don't be like the woman doctor who tells men that she's in "health management" rather than fling her profession at them outright. Contrived or demeaning ploys are unnecessary. If you're a doctor, say you're a doctor with pride, *but express comparable respect for what he does.* (That's if you *feel* it. If you have to fake respect for what he does—and that's an important part of him—you're with the wrong person.)

What you want to avoid is getting into a deadly "Can You Top This?" contest, with him matching your credentials and achievements against his. Give him an inside look at your world without stirring up his natural competitiveness. When you talk about your work, stick to the work itself—how it's done, why it absorbs you, what's challenging about it—and don't get into your surpassing excellence at it, hoping he'll kiss your Fiorucci boots in admiration. You'll find his admiration much easier to come by when you don't solicit it directly.

You may feel entitled to trade in the world of love strictly on the basis of your job or career success, without throwing into the package any of the traditional womanly things—making him a home-cooked meal occasionally, helping him with his problems, bolstering his self-esteem. But when you shun caretaking completely, you do yourself as great a disservice as the woman who gives a man too much too soon. She straps herself to get a commitment—and you don't invest enough.

Angela, a young radio news reporter who keeps a killing schedule, can't understand why her boyfriend says she's too independent for him. "He thinks I don't need anything from him," she complains, "because he sees that I've got it together, that I'm making it on my own and can take care of myself." She says nothing about taking care of *him*, which doesn't figure into her plans at all.

Like many women in high-powered, demanding jobs, Angela is afraid to do anything that smacks of old-time nurturing, because she doesn't want to get locked into doting on a man at the expense of her career. To contain her relationship, she gives it as little attention as possible, and then wonders why it doesn't thrive on neglect.

Remember this: The only problem with the old-time nurturing was the *degree*. In the past, giving 100 percent was uncomfortable for women; today, getting 0 percent is uncomfortable for men. Like most of our terrors, the sacrifices and compromises we fear we'll have to make for a good loving relationship are often greater in our heads than they are in real life.

Many a busy career woman who couldn't find the time to share her life with a man suddenly found the time when it became important enough to her. Linda, a doctor who'd had a relationship-on-the-run with a man in her medical-school class, began to miss Dave after he left for a residency at a hospital in Denver. Although it pressed her, she took time off from her own residency in Chicago to get out to Denver to see him. Dave did the traveling after that, and the relationship flourished. But when Linda said something about a commitment, Dave's answer (and he meant it seriously) was "When we both have the time."

Linda realized that if she wanted Dave, a lateral move was in order. She transferred out of her pediatric residency in Chicago to a rotating one at the hospital in Denver, and married Dave during the Thanksgiving break in their schedules.

Being flexible about career choices and mobility doesn't make your work less important than his; it merely makes you more adaptable. Romantic success often hinges on accessibility. If you have fears and anxieties about accommodating a man, even while yearning for an intimate relationship, make one small change at a time in your workaholic patterns or life-style. These changes—taking a weeknight off to go out, cooking dinner for a date, quarantining the raging clutter in your home— won't stall your drive to the top. Being less obsessive won't turn you into a fat, plant-watering hausfrau overnight. Cultivate the knack for balancing work with a loving relationship, and use it to your advantage.

4. *The Openness Myth*

It drives you up a wall that all he wants to talk about are football scores, his college exploits, the latest sci-fi movie, or his skill at interoffice finagling. You want to talk about the things that matter—feelings, relationships, Life. The superficiality of his conversation bores and frustrates you. He's intelligent and educated, then why can't he be deep? You want him to trade confidences with you, to be more open about his private passions, to disclose how he really feels. So you start pushing him to reveal what's inside himself—and you push him away.

Be honest about it: When you complain that a man is not in touch with his feelings, you're talking about his feelings for *you*. You'd like him to come right out and say how much he cares, to tell you why he appreciates and admires you, to voice approval and encouragement. What *he* calls "openness"—baring his insecurities about himself—is distasteful to you. You want him to be close-mouthed about his worries and loose-tongued about his love. But you don't realize that the danger he attaches to falling in love—entrapment in a smothering relationship, or betrayal by rejection or deceit—is one of the things he worries about most.

Rushing his defenses will only intensify his fear of entrapment or betrayal. As much as it may gall you, you'll have to move toward openness slowly if you want it to mean anything. Instant openness, like instant love, is often deceptive. How can he be in love with you if he hasn't taken the time to find out who you are? "If I'd thought he knew me well enough to care for me, I'd have been flattered," says a twenty-nine-year-old nurse of her ill-fated relationship with a man who fell "madly in love" with her on their first date. "He wrote me passionate letters and left flowers at my door," she recalls, "but he was courting this image of me as an angel of mercy. Before me, he was in love with another angel—Kate Jackson on TV."

Most men prefer to play their cards much closer to their vests—too close for comfort. It's annoying that you should have to tease a man out of his defenses when yours have already crumbled. His skittishness can make you feel unwanted. But remember, you don't have the same ingrained fear of intimacy that he does. Because closeness spells danger for him, it may be a reflex action when he backs away from it or fends it off by being "superficial." You can't take it personally if he doesn't want to become involved as readily as you do. Blame the culture or biology for a low trick, but, by virtue of being a woman, you'll have to convince him that you're as trustworthy as a parish priest in a confessional before he'll reveal his innermost feelings.

The dating period is the time to enjoy the excitement of the chase and to luxuriate in discovery. It's not a time to wallow in openness like two participants in a group therapy session. *Give romance a chance.* Don't think that sex, if you choose to have it, gives you the right to press him into immediate service as a husband. Overstepping certain carefully drawn lines between friendship and love at this point can signal entrapment to him and send him scurrying.

While you're working to gain his trust (with a chisel, not a sledgehammer), use your network as a shoulder to cry on about your problems or as a cheering section for your triumphs; and when you're with him, be your most sparkling, scintillating self. Laugh at his jokes (even if you've heard them before) and concentrate on being good company. One woman who used this technique found that the "superficial" man she'd met at work (and later married) was far brainier, deeper, and more cultured than she'd ever imagined. On the job, he'd confine himself to talking about football and office politics instead of his real interests—music, art, theater, Life—because he didn't want to seem too highbrow for his co-workers.

This may seem unfair to you, but I think that a free demonstration of tenderness—*with no strings attached*—is a must on your part if you hope to attain genuine openness in a relationship today. Male sensitivity is still a relatively new idea. A friend of mine once confided that she had to give her thirty-five-year-old boyfriend "human-being lessons" before he dropped his gruffness and became more loving. Some men who are perfectly capable of caring (although you'd never know it) need tenderness training. You may be grooming one for a committed relationship with someone else, but that's a better risk than going nowhere with him yourself. And it's not unlikely that a woman powerful and secure enough to become a man's mentor in intimacy may wind up marrying one of her protegés.

There's no doubt that it can be a potent aphrodisiac to a man when you offer him compassion, reassurance, and understanding while keeping your own need for babying under control. But don't attempt to do this without guiding yourself by the "sweat equity" rule. If too prolonged, the one-sided giving of tenderness can turn you into a resentful burnout or a victim of the classic tenderness trap that claimed generations of women before you. After your free demonstration of tenderness, show him you're human, too.

When you engage in self-disclosure, however, make an enormous effort to restrain yourself from going too far. *Edit your story*. At the heart of romance is a kernel of mystery. The current compulsion to be totally open and honest about every piece of their past lives has created the biggest hurdle for lovers who are trying to build an enduring relationship. In their eagerness to show themselves as they really are (or, more accurately, to gain sympathy or relief from guilt), they reveal jarring things about themselves that may not be at all relevant to their current involvement and are better left unsaid. By being open *to a fault*, they shatter their ideal image too quickly and impair basic trust.

Let's suppose you've begun dating a man who thinks infidelity is dirty pool (they usually do, if you're the one who's doing it). How's he going to take it when you launch into a vivid account of the three extramarital affairs you had during your sexually frustrating seven-year marriage? In his head he can understand why you cheated on your husband and wouldn't with him; but in his *gut*, the seeds of suspicion about your integrity have been planted.

Why jeopardize a new relationship by revealing unpleasant secrets about yourself that a man might not be able to handle? Jocelyn, a twenty-seven-year-old secretary, thought she could gain the sympathy of a man she was dating by divulging how she'd tried to commit suicide after her last long-term relationship ended. Having had successful therapy, Jocelyn felt confident that she'd never go off the deep end again, but the man she was seeing was disturbed by what he'd heard. His feelings for Jocelyn were tinged with doubts about her stability, and although they enjoyed a long dating relationship, he never let himself become seriously involved with her.

Wanting someone to love you warts and all doesn't preclude using discretion about which warts to expose. I think the two most important criteria are (1) how the information will be judged by the man (infidelity might horrify one man and be laughed off by another) and (2) whether concealing something poses a bigger threat to the relationship or to the man personally than disclosure.

A dramatic example is the touchy subject of herpes, the incurable viral infection that carriers can transmit during sex. Many experts and sufferers alike believe you shouldn't tell a person initially that you have herpes, but should wait until the relationship is serious and heading toward commitment. But if you try that, you're risking rejection far down the line when it will hurt a lot worse than initially (*Time* magazine reported that one fiancé so informed walked out on his bride-to-be a month before their scheduled wedding).

Because it involves actual harm to someone, herpes is one of the few "secrets" you can't afford *not* to reveal after you've established trust but before you're moving toward commitment. Keeping silent too long is even worse than talking too soon, because it magnifies the element of deceit. (Most people can accept bad news better than the hurt of being lied to.) Openness at an optimum midpoint will spare you the ordeal of living a lie that could come to light explosively at any time. And if this man senses how much you could mean to him (and understands how the transmission of herpes can be controlled), the chances are good that your honesty will encourage him to continue the relationship.

Unlike the disclosure of herpes, much of what passes for openness today is a form of self-indulgence rather than an expression of true honesty or concern for the other person. As you become experienced in relationships, you often find that damaging information you once thought so important to divulge becomes less important the more at peace you are with these matters yourself. Inner peace is just about the most alluring quality anyone can have. If time and your network aren't doing it, see a therapist to help you exorcise those demons that may have no place in a dating relationship.

Once a relationship is established, you can let him get in closer to see the hidden springs that make you tick. Even then, you may not want to divulge certain past experiences that don't concern him directly. Revelations about the way you were are not nearly so important as careful honesty about how you are now—your views, preferences, feelings. This kind of self-disclosure is not only more interesting than unadulterated gobs of oral history, it's more powerful. It's being straight, not shocking, that keeps a viable romance alive and well.

5. *Platonic Plus*

Behind most women who have succeeded at love is at least one platonic friendship with a man. Variously described as a "buddy," a "confidant," and, wryly, a "friend in the enemy camp," platonic males are often credited with playing a key role in women's romantic success.

A platonic is a man who offers you all the comforts of a sexual relationship except sex. You can go out on the town with him, take him to parties as your escort, talk to him for hours on the phone—and never do anything more passionate with him than kiss him goodnight on the cheek.

Maybe you tried sex with him and wish you hadn't. Maybe he's too close to home—the ex-husband of your best girlfriend, for example—and sex with him, because you're not curious anymore or he doesn't turn you on, seems vaguely incestuous and taboo. Or maybe it's a matter of self-defense: You know it's not going to pan out with him (your personalities don't mesh; he's not ready), and you'd rather preserve your pristine friendship than turn it into a messy affair. Whatever the reason, a platonic is someone who matters greatly to you, but he matters more out of bed than in it.

Why is he so critical to your success? Because he's a hedge against desperation. He's someone who can keep you from running scared when you're on the verge, or prevent you from screwing up a main-chance relationship by doing rash things (you can call *him* and not lose an inch of ground when you're battling Ma Bell).

A platonic can also be invaluable to you as your window on the male world. As a man who knows the mysterious workings of his own defenses against love, he can explain them to you and interpret baffling behavior that might otherwise lead you astray.

Jill, now married to Herb, says that a knowing platonic helped save her relationship with Herb when she didn't know which end was up. Jill and Herb went boating one weekend with Nina and Peter, Jill's closest friends, who were meeting Herb for the first time. Although Herb was newly divorced and dating others, Jill felt he really cared for her. His callous behavior that weekend made no sense to Jill at all. "He embarrassed me in front of my friends," Jill recalls, "by giving them the impression that I was just another filly in his stable. I was mortified when Nina and Peter got me aside and said, 'Hey, listen, Jill, you'd better find out where this guy is coming from. If he's just into a phase, that's one thing. But if you're never going to be more than an also-ran to him, let him tell you that now.' "

As soon as they were on dry land, Jill consulted her platonic. What she wanted to know was, Had Herb misrepresented his position to Nina and Peter or had he misrepresented it to her? Was he using her or did he care for her as much as she thought he did?

Putting himself in Herb's place, the platonic gave Jill his reading of the situation: Herb cared for Jill, judging by the way he acted when they were alone, but he wanted to make sure her friends knew he wasn't ready to settle down in case the relationship didn't last. Herb was trying to save face because he didn't know how much Jill cared for him. He felt he had to downplay their involvement to protect himself—what if Jill had told Nina and Peter that *she* wasn't serious? Women, the platonic told her, have no monopoly on self-doubt.

The platonic's insights helped Jill gently turn a corner with Herb instead of angrily pushing him too far. It wasn't until they'd started living together and were reminiscing about their dating days that Jill discovered how right the platonic had been. Herb admitted that his flamboyance about other women was a function of his insecurity with Jill.

Sometimes a very intuitive woman friend can decipher the male psyche for you this way, but conjecture is rarely as accurate as recognition.

Besides mind reading and companionship, a platonic can be indispensable to you when you're trying to stir up the jealousies of a man who needs the incentive of competition. Does this imply calculation or ruthlessness on your part? Not necessarily. You may or may not arrange to bump into your platonic or have him call you at the very time your date happens to be there—the choice is yours. You can depend on luck or you can use your ingenuity to conjure up your platonic when his calls or presence will have the most telling effect on a date. Try to hurry through these three-way encounters with a convincing show of embarrassment. As long as you don't dawdle, your date can't accuse you of rudeness or insensitivity; he can only be impressed with your popularity.

Even if he remains mute and invisible to a date, your platonic can crop up as an unnervingly mysterious figure in your conversations. Not that you'd ever do anything so gauche as to talk about a platonic himself. But what's to stop you from describing the hilarious party or trendy little nouvelle-cuisine restaurant that a purposely vague "friend" took you to? Let your date's imagination do the rest. This is one of those times when the charitable act of sharing an experience with another can accrue to your benefit.

6. Safe Sex

Just as a nonsexual relationship with a platonic can help you do better with a live one, so can a sexual relationship with a "safe" man—one you're in no danger of falling in love with and who won't fall in love with you. A sexually safe man must be attractive and challenging enough to arouse you physically but pose no threat to a serious relationship, because he's unthinkable as a permanent partner. He's off limits because of color, class, age, or some other barrier that both of you deem insuperable except for a friendly, albeit passionate, affair. You may fantasize about being married to him (and, incidentally, men imagine what married life would be like with almost every woman they sleep with, too), but since you both know you won't try to act this fantasy out, the affair is self-limiting.

Although this restrictiveness can be irksome, it won't become excruciating if you keep your objectives firmly fixed in your mind. This is an *auxiliary* affair, nothing more, and it can be a great boon when you're trying to develop a serious relationship with another man. Since you're not being deprived of sex—and don't underrate safe sex as a valuable source of reassurance, release, affection, and experience—you'll have a more relaxed and confident perspective on sex as it develops in a dating relationship. When other women, who don't have a safety man, are champing at the bit for sex, you'll have the fortitude to delay sleeping with a date until you think the timing is right. You'll also be more patient with a man who's having a bout of impotence, a common occurrence, and not give up prematurely as some women do. And unlike so many "deprived" women who succumb to fatal outbursts of anger, you'll be able to bide your time sweetly when a date temporarily pulls back from intimacy or is openly juggling his options.

Kept within its parameters, safe sex can be a factor in that marginal difference known as a "winning edge."

The Bottom Line

"You can't buy futures in relationships," Hilary once told me when we were discussing her remarkable success in both business and love. Divorced in her thirties, Hilary took an entry-level job with a huge corporation and within ten years was made national head of public relations. Shortly after joining the company, she met a branch director who left his wife for her (Hilary made him leave *first*), and they've lived together happily ever since.

But after all this time, Hilary doesn't think her relationship is completely safe from harm. She worries about getting hit with such things as infidelity or waning desire. Like many successful people, she focuses confidently on what lies ahead but makes allowances for unwelcome surprises. She aims continually for the best without assuming that the worst can't happen. Uncertainty, she says, is the one thing you can depend on in life. When she created a stir by unexpectedly taking a year off from work to concentrate full-time on her relationship, Hilary offered the explanation that a commitment is not a guaranty ("You can't buy futures in relationships").

If a commitment doesn't guarantee your future with a man, you can hardly expect guaranties *going into* a relationship. Yet in these days of sex-before-love, more is at stake than ever before. Losing carries bigger penalties, and for many women there's a conflict between what they know about guarantees against loss and what they feel. A woman who's coming off a bruising relationship will say to the next man, knowing she's chasing him away as she utters the words, "I'm not having sex again unless there's a commitment."

Even if this message isn't verbally expressed, many women feel that when sex is offered, a commitment should be the bottom line. This feeling may be fostered strictly by their own need for monogamy (a trait that was genetically implanted in women, some experts say, to improve the quality of their offspring and that women are evolving out of but haven't shaken off entirely). Acting on their inner urgings rather than any rational basis, some women are angrier and more embittered than they need to be when a relationship doesn't work out. They expected more than was promised, more than they had a right to expect, and that's what makes them experience disappointment as a crushing failure.

As indispensable as a "win some, lose some" attitude is to success in the business world, that's how invaluable it is to success in love. All of the women who've made it say that they learned to take false starts in stride and accept uncertainty as the challenge of romance. They tried to minimize their risks by looking hard before they leaped and by taking their losses early. Once they leaped, they wouldn't let their own or others' pressures for a commitment force them into blunders or rob them of their enjoyment of the game. By pouring their energies into creating a better relationship each time around, they *earned* the bottom line through performance.

MORAL: You have to keep your line in the water until the big fish bites.

6

The Semipermanent Relationship

W e've now come to a watershed event: A string of consecutive dates with one man has blossomed into a serious (or at least steady) relationship. You're not alone anymore. There's a man in your life who takes you out regularly, cares about you, satisfies your sexual needs, and does everything else that a partner in a love relationship can be expected to do, except— except that he's *not* the Right One. Does that mean that you're wasting your time? Never! This is your first extended opportunity to develop your lovemanship skills in earnest—to learn what works and doesn't work for you on a continuing basis; what you must have and what you can't stand; what you can rise above and what'll put you under.

You might want to think of this as an interim relationship, although you probably won't have the sense to think of it that way until you're well out of it and into the next one. It has that phase-related quality—on the ladder of love, it occupies a place in the middle range between entry level and the top.

It can happen when you're nineteen and you get involved with him because it's the perfect college romance. It's perfect for *now*, but who knows what each of you will want in a partner five years down the pike? Or it can happen when you're thirty-five and just coming out of the "crazy period" following your divorce. You're tired of the sexual kaleidoscope and you want to settle down with one man—*any* man who'll give you the comfort and security of a steady thing while you're adjusting to being a single working mother afoot in the big, hard world. Or it can happen *whenever* the need for an exclusive relationship crowds out the factors implicit in its impermanence.

The New Courtship

To be fair about it, I think the semipermanent relationship deserves a place in history. It should be seen in a sociological perspective rather than as some misbegotten enterprise that didn't work out. The semipermanent relationship—one that evolves out of a particular stage in your life, burns brightly for a while, and disappears—is a recent phenomenon that has taken the place of the old-style courtship. It's a serious relationship that affords the feeling of permanence for the time being. In the Fifties, this kind of relationship (minus the sex) amounted to "going steady" and was usually a prelude to marriage. But the new courtship is a collection of these relationships strung out over a period of years. It's a "multiple courtship" consisting of any number of affairs of varying length, all fairly intense and exclusive, leading up to a really permanent attachment.

Most semipermanent relationships are a curious mixture of security and frustration. Even while you're in them, you're aware that you have only the illusion of a commitment. While you don't have to worry about not having someone, you sense that this particular someone isn't right for the long haul. Deep down, you know that this relationship has a limited life because it's either missing some essential ingredient or laboring against some external barrier.

Losing a semipermanent partner is inevitable, but sometimes you get so dependent on the sheer convenience of having him around that you're devastated when he leaves. This shell shock can be avoided if, when you enter into a semipermanent relationship, you acknowledge its limitations to yourself and resist the temptation to try to make it more than what it is. Appreciate it for serving a worthy purpose—answering your need for intimacy at a certain time in your life while increasing your power and ability to love. Don't live in fear of its demise, *but always be prepared for it to end.* Eventually, you'll be glad that it didn't work out and that it paved the way to greater romantic success.

Semipermanent relationships run the gamut from those obviously destined to be short-lived (you wouldn't want them any longer) to those that may go on for years and start falsely acquiring the look of permanence before they crash into their own impossibility and self-destruct. *But the game goes on.* To get from amateur status to the world-class league, you've got to analyze these relationships to understand where they fall short of the mark and what they're telling you to avoid or look for the next time around. Ergo, I present these three groups of semipermanents and some chronicles of women who toughed them out and went on to win in the game of love. It isn't necessary or even advisable for you to experience all three types personally, but an understanding of them is a kingpin of the course.

1. The Wellington

To outside observers, this relationship of convenience could easily be mistaken for the real thing, but, like the Wellington diamond, it's only a contrived imitation. It's pleasant and comfortable but flatter than stale Perrier because it lacks, in one woman's phrase, "the sharp edge." Both of you want an easy relationship without stress, so you tacitly enter into a conspiracy of needs. What you come up with is an artificial attachment that observes all the rituals of a real relationship— daily phone calls, continuous dates, regular sex—without the encumbrance of genuine feeling.

Tammy began seeing Burt when her relationship with a married man was going nowhere at a painfully slow pace. She saw Burt as a way out, and that was all that mattered: "I couldn't have cared less that he was too old for me or that he had a drinking problem or that he came from a dirt-poor background in Tennessee—Burt was *free*. He was a widower, a kindly, courtly southern gentleman who had recently lost his eldest daughter in an automobile accident. He needed me as much as I needed him. He revered women, and he was attentive and generous. After a year of sneaking around in a crummy affair, I was delighted to be with a man who would cater to me and treat me with dignity."

The relationship was purposeful but synthetic from the start. Burt was a fiftyish church elder and Tammy was a thirtyish sex therapist, and goodwill alone wasn't enough to bridge their separate worlds. "I always felt that we were grossly mismatched," Tammy recalls, "especially when he dragged me to things like AA meetings or sales conventions where I was the odd one out. He was a nice man, but alien to me I had to get stoned on pot to have sex with him. It was the only way I could be intimate without desire."

Still, the relationship had strengths that Tammy remembers fondly. "I met Burt right before Thanksgiving, and I was desolate at the thought of having to spend another holiday alone. Then Burt invited me to his daughter-in-law's home for Thanksgiving dinner. Burt had the kind of family I'd always wanted— a big, close-knit family, very warm and loving. I could relate to his children, who were more like me than Burt, and we became very friendly. It was wonderful to have that feeling of belonging. Burt was the patriarch. That was the most seductive thing about him—he went out of his way to get me to depend on him, and he was always *there*."

They saw each other for about six months. But while the relationship was exclusive on both sides because Burt insisted on that from the beginning, it was distinctly a Wellington.

Neither Tammy nor Burt could reveal their true feelings. Tammy pretended to love Burt, although what she really felt was a kind of tame fondness. She was frustrated because she couldn't talk to him about her deepest concerns. Burt had little interest in her work other than to brag about her professional success to his friends. Their conversations centered mostly around people Burt knew in the AA program or experiences he'd lived through, and Tammy was bored. There was also the problem of sex. It was too mechanical for Tammy, and she constantly had to devise ways to cut back on the frequency and spare herself guilt.

As for Burt, he secretly thought Tammy was too independent and elusive, but he applied himself to the relationship conscientiously and busied himself with the formalities. He called his "sweetheart" every day like clockwork, ran errands for her, bought her gifts. But grief over his daughter's death, coupled with mounting business pressures, finally caught up with Burt, and he fell off the wagon with a loud thud.

Tammy remembers their bizarre Lost Weekend. "He was late picking me up one Saturday night, and I was worried because he hadn't called. That wasn't like him. I called around, and no one seemed to know where he was. While I was pacing about the bedroom, I happened to look out the window and was astonished to see Burt's car in my driveway with the lights on and Burt apparently asleep at the wheel. It was impossible to know how long he'd been there. I ran downstairs and went out to him. He was in a stupor. I rapped on the car window and he shook himself awake. He stared at me blankly with this insipid look on his face and staggered out of the car, holding a beer can in his hand. It was snowing hard, and the wet flakes falling on his skin surprised him. 'Oh, is it raining?' he asked me. I marveled at how he'd driven across town in that condition and had reached me alive!"

Tammy got Burt inside and tried to sober him up. "He wasn't an abusive drunk," she recalls, "but he had scared me silly. I hadn't encountered anything like this before and didn't know how to deal with it." She let him sleep it off, and Burt woke up a couple of hours later, abjectly apologetic and insistent that he make it up to Tammy and take her out.

"Like a dope, I agreed," says Tammy. "When I got inside the car, I thought I was going to be sick. It smelled like a brewery. Empty beer cans were strewn all over the back seat. I didn't even know that Burt liked beer—I thought he was a whiskey drinker—but then I figured out that the six-packs were easier to drink in the car nonstop. He must have been driving with a can welded to his hand.

"We stopped for a late dinner and went back to his place. As soon as we got there, he made a beeline to another stash of six-packs in the refrigerator and began guzzling them compulsively. When he collapsed on his bed, I flushed what was left of the beer down the toilet. Later, he tried to make love to me, but he couldn't because he kept hiccuping spasmodically from all that drinking. It was pathetic and ludicrous at the same time."

Burt was chagrined by this episode and clung to a tenuous sobriety for the next few months. He tried to be more attentive than ever to Tammy, but she realized there was too much wrong with the relationship for it ever to amount to anything. She let it recede into the background of her life, concentrating on her work and her network of friends.

Spurious as her Wellington was, Tammy would never have junked it without a real diamond to take its place. But what most women in such relationships don't realize is that the men who are in them are not fooled by the lack of authenticity either. Presented with a good excuse for ending the relationship or with another woman who offers more genuine feeling, they'll vanish as all transient lovers do through that famous trapdoor.

Tammy never suspected that she'd be seeing Burt for the last time when she went off to Puerto Rico with a woman colleague to attend a weeklong seminar. She assumed that Burt would be waiting for her at the airport on her return, loyal and affectionate as an old sheepdog. It occurred to her that her going away was a threat to Burt's security, but she thought she'd succeeded in allaying his fears. Tammy wasn't interested in seeking out other men; all she wanted was a working vacation.

Given her good intentions, Tammy was dismayed by how easily she succumbed to temptation. On her first night away, she found herself in bed with a sophisticated but jaded high roller on a gambling trip—a Lizard who tried to bed down Tammy's companion after he'd slept with Tammy. Humiliated by this experience, Tammy came home with a deeper appreciation for Burt's earnest, plodding brand of attentiveness.

"When he wasn't at the airport to meet me, my first thought was that he'd been drinking again," Tammy remembers. "But when I called him up, he was perfectly sober. He hemmed and hawed before he finally blurted that he'd found a new girlfriend. I think he hit the panic button while I was away, and it was a matter of 'dump or *be* dumped.' But mostly, he knew that our relationship wasn't right, so he just seized the opportunity to bail out."

Losing a Wellington can be a jolt, but the loss doesn't involve the same rage and bitterness as the death of love. It's a light slap on the cheek compared to getting your head bashed in with a crowbar. Relatively harmless because it lacks the fire and vividness of a real connection, it nevertheless has a positive value for the woman who is trying to learn how to balance love with the other parts of her life.

Says Tammy, who subsequently went through several other semipermanent relationships and is now happily married: "Before Burt, I couldn't have a romance without getting swallowed up alive in it. Burt represented the opposite extreme—there was nothing so compelling about our affair that it intruded in my life in any way. I think some women need to go from one extreme to the other in order to find the right trade-off between giving and holding back. Most of us don't know our parameters instinctively—they have to be tested out."

Boring, flat, and stale as it may be, a Wellington should not be underrated as a crucial part of that testing-out experience. If you're in that awkward stage in your development when you can't afford to invest fully in a relationship, an economical and serviceable Wellington may see you through.

2. *The Half-Loaf*

Basically, the Half-Loaf is a compromise relationship. You know that he isn't quite all you want, but you figure he's better than nothing. Now, while every relationship involves *some* compromise, the Half-Loaf is impossibly lopsided. The missing half is so overwhelming, so constantly on your mind, that the conflict it causes will never be resolved. Like a bicycle with a flat tire, the Half-Loaf can only go so far.

Unlike the Wellington, a Half-Loaf has some real passion in it. It's a more honest relationship, and the sparks fly more often, both in bed and in heated argument. The common factor in all true Half-Loaves is a nagging, ever-present feeling that this essentially decent man is somehow lacking. The disparity between what you want and what he can give you—a glitch that could be financial, sexual, intellectual, etc.—is one that no personal best, yours or his, can reconcile. Far from being hidden, the glitch is usually as glaringly obvious as frontal nudity. Averting your eyes accomplishes nothing except the purchase of time.

Half-Loaves often fail on the basis of a lack of "chemistry" or physical attraction even when sex, perversely, may be uncommonly good. But the physical side of the relationship goes far beyond sex. He might be the most accomplished lover ever to have bedded you down, and yet the desire for him doesn't stick. You don't feel that sweet craving for him; you don't fantasize about him in the middle of your board meeting. Buried somewhere in your genes and in our upbringing is a very basic, individual set of preferences: blond hair and blue eyes, long legs, smooth skin, strong hands, wiry frame, hairy/hairless chest, older/younger-looking, etc. While these feelings may seem very arbitrary to us, to deny them their proper place in the love equation is to ask for trouble.

My friend Marla is a successful, hard-driving account executive who now lives in the chic California community of Westwood. Petite and elegant, very social, Marla always told me that she adored dynamic men who were Nordic-looking: tall, blond, and slim, with flat, hairless chests. So it came as a surprise when she announced that she'd been seeing Gene. What could possibly have attracted her in this spectacularly dull, mild-mannered accountant? Gene was stocky and swarthy, with pecs that resembled—in Marla's words—"boobs" and a chest like the Black Forest. Unlike Marla, Gene felt uncomfortable at parties, especially the big bashes thrown by the ad agency for which they both worked. Compared with Marla's silk and fine linen clothes, Gene's closet could only be described as Polyester Paradise.

What drew Marla and Gene together was the love they shared of good theater and good restaurants, plus Gene's irresistible devotion to Marla. No sooner would she say she wanted something than he'd get it for her, whether it was a glass of wine or a piece of Louis Vuitton luggage. And technically, Marla had to admit, Gene was the best lover she'd ever had—exquisitely attuned to what she needed. But try as she would, she couldn't get past his unappealing looks and tacky wardrobe, as well as the dullness of his personality and his lack of brainpower. On some deep, unspoken level, Marla couldn't help picturing Gene as Godzilla in a leisure suit.

About four months into their affair, Marla began complaining of the frequent fights she'd been having with Gene. "It's so frustrating," she sighed. "I finally found a man who'll knock himself out to please me, but the packaging is all wrong. Every time I make suggestions or buy him something nice to wear— you know, kind of steer him in the right direction—he gets bent out of shape and tells me how shallow I am to be so concerned with appearance."

Gene was asserting the traditional male prerogative in romance: *A man who falls in love with a woman thereby removes her objections to him.* He almost had Marla fooled. Certainly he had her confused. "I feel guilty as hell," she confided. "I really shouldn't let Gene's looks get in the way, but they do. He's just not the sort of guy you show off at a cocktail party or have wild imaginings about. Sexually, I can't bring myself to do anything for him. He's great in bed—he pushes all the right buttons—and I lie there, coming like crazy but completely passive. To be honest, every time we make love I have to forget that I'm doing it with *him*."

It took Marla another month to accept the inevitability of her physical preferences. For her, Gene's "packaging" was a *fixed* priority that went much deeper than the clothes on his back. Even when he made the grand gesture of refurbishing his wardrobe, Gene was still *Gene* to Marla—Godzilla in a Bill Blass suit. Undressed, he appealed to her not a whit more.

As Marla discovered in her next affair—this time with a tall, lean, fair-skinned blond go-getter—desire dances to its own beat. *Listen to the music!* If you have to pretend it's playing when it isn't, what you've got is a Half-Loaf. Fine tuning might make the relationship somewhat more palatable, but it won't make it whole.

Isn't it possible for a woman who goes batty over tall, lean blonds to fall passionately in love with a dark little bull of a man who turns her on through the force of his charismatic personality or intellectual brilliance? Yes, but if she's genuinely turned on by him, then his other qualities have rendered his physical traits relatively unimportant—a minor glitch—and it's not really a Half-Loaf anymore, is it?

The problem is, we all have some priorities that are like stretch marks—they're more *fixed* than we care to admit. A Half-Loaf arises when we try to disown some given that we unalterably value in a man—looks, money, drive, achievement, a sense of humor—and the lack of it just won't go away.

Why do women hoodwink themselves into settling for a marginal Half-Loaf that goes against their own grain? Most Half-Loafers are desperate. Some don't know their own priorities and have to learn them through trial and error. Still others, like Marla, know what they like but somehow feel ashamed for clinging to values that people (often the men they reject) call "shallow."

Whether prompted by fear, ignorance, or self-doubt, a Half-Loaf can be a supremely valuable experience. When a woman who's willing to trade down finds out that she can't, there's often nowhere to go but up.

If a man is physically appealing to you but unacceptable because of his image (tacky clothes, weird hairdo), the glitch may or may not be fatal. There's hope if a man dresses wretchedly only because he doesn't know any better. The Look, as we've seen, can be acquired. But image-doctoring won't cure the disease if his grungy T-shirts and Hell's Angel–style boots are a personal statement of deeply ingrained attitudes or social class. You have to discern how closely his image bespeaks the inner man. If the medium is the message (he dresses like a creep because he *is* a creep), it's useless to tamper with the packaging unless you honestly like the product.

The deficiencies (differences, really) that make for a Half-Loaf range across the whole spectrum of human nature and experience—everything from the wrong taste in movies to the wrong religion. But there are no absolutes. Some Fellini fanatics can merge handily with some sitcom lovers, as can some WASPs with some Jewish American Princesses. Again, it's only when the glitch is an overriding concern that wipes out a basic congruence in all other areas—physical, material, emotional, intellectual—that you have to worry.

Some barriers exist more in the minds of others than in yours or his, but that may not stop them from being insuperable all the same. Interfaith relationships are a good example. While they're less hazardous than they used to be, don't underestimate the strength of hard-line family pressures. Tolerance for a religious difference is often easier to summon than the courage to withstand parental disapproval. Says Eileen, a working-class Irish Catholic law student, of her star-crossed romance with a classmate whose father was a municipal court judge: "I broke up with Mark when he wouldn't take me home to meet his parents during spring break. It enraged me that I was a *shiksa* to him—someone you slept with but didn't take seriously. Then Mark told me how his parents had been sticking it to him because of me, and I realized that he wasn't a callous bastard, after all. His intentions *were* good—they just weren't good enough."

Another woman, a sophisticated divorced Jewish college prof in her forties, was heading toward remarriage with her rough-hewn, unmistakably Gentile boyfriend until they had to make their first public appearance as a couple at her nephew's bar mitzvah. "For weeks I agonized over how to make John more presentable to my relatives and friends," Diane says, "and then the truth hit me: I'm ashamed of this man. The affair came to an end after that because I realized that I couldn't change John's small-town *goyishe* sensibility—his fondness for Spam, loud plaids, and Early American furniture."

Diane has since lucked out with a Jewish think-tank type she adores and is proud to present to her social circle. Her advice to other women? "After the novelty of a radical departure from the familiar wears off," she says, "ask yourself if you're not going to miss those shared traditions and customs and

verbal expressions and everyday things you enjoy with someone from your own set. To throw that over, you've got to
either be very flexible or love the guy a lot. It's not something
you can successfully rationalize away."

To show you that love *can* conquer all (providing, of course,
that the "all" is negotiable), let me tell you about my friend
Harriet and her boyfriend, Jim. For them, the glitch wasn't
religion but rather a quantum gap in education and social status.
Harriet is a thirty-two-year-old social worker who's highly
regarded in academic circles and has published papers in major
journals. Her looks are marred by an acne-scarred skin and a
broad, diet-proof frame, but her captivating warmth makes
you forget all that within moments of meeting her.

Harriet was standing near the hors d'oeuvres table at a colleague's party one night when an astonishingly handsome,
thirtyish man (Jim) struck up a conversation with her just as
she was about to pop a giant, dip-slathered mushroom into
her mouth. Assuming that Jim was a fellow professional, Harriet was taken aback when he identified himself as a mushroom
grower (it was an established family business) whose handiwork
Harriet was sampling.

"Jim had gravitated toward me because he thought I was
approachable," says Harriet. "I liked him immediately. I couldn't
believe anyone so good-looking could be that unspoiled. Compared to all the neurotic men I'd known, Jim was refreshingly
happy, uncomplicated, and eager to please. The snob in me
said, 'A *mushroom grower?*' But the woman in me said, 'Why not?' "

Harriet and Jim began dating, fell into a serious relationship,
and ended up living together. Jim's lack of formal education
(Harriet had two graduate degrees whereas Jim hadn't gone
beyond the twelfth grade) made Harriet defensive at first, but
she gradually realized that the education gap was unimportant
in the scheme of their relationship: "When people get to know
Jim, they stop wondering what we have in common. He's
intuitive about people and life, and his perceptions make up

for what he hasn't read in books. Not that he isn't well read. But what's more important is that he's genuinely interested in me and what I do, and I find him fascinating because he's special. Hey, I've got a lot of friends in my field to dish with about fancy abstractions; but when I want to talk to someone about the things that matter personally to me, Jim is the only one who's personally *concerned.*"

In effect, Harriet had traded down on education and status for the sexual turn-on of youth and good looks, and for the warmth and insights of a truly caring man. *That* people could understand. What Harriet's friends (friends?) found more puzzling was Jim's attraction to a plain-looking woman who was neither rich nor powerful. To explain this phenomenon, Harriet came up with her "wounded-bird theory." Says Harriet: "Men and women relate on the basis of self-esteem. A handsome man who has confidence in himself usually seeks out an equally attractive woman. But a handsome man who *doesn't* have confidence in himself—he's been shot down by early life experience or whatever like a wounded bird—that's another story. Now you've got someone who doesn't care so much about looks. He's vulnerable to the woman who can restore his sense of self-esteem. Jim is that way—a very shy, sensitive person who needs strength in a woman but would be easily intimidated by a strong, *beautiful* woman who'd overpower him."

Whether you buy Harriet's theory or not—and, personally, I think it makes some sense—be aware that a less-than-beautiful woman whose physical standards are high has historically been most successful in love with a man whose handsomeness is leavened with a little humility.

Here's another example of a couple who negotiated a glitch—financial, this time—and turned a potential Half-Loaf into a very satisfying, committed relationship. Joan, an ambitious New York magazine editor, had been married for fifteen years to a big name in the literary world. At the time that his eye wandered toward a Hollywood starlet, Joan's husband was pulling down a fast $200,000 a year as a novelist and screenwriter.

After the divorce, while she was still a struggling assistant editor (her ex-husband had gone broke on starlets, booze, and bad investments), Joan went to a screening of *Jaws* and met Tony, an underpaid film critic for a local newspaper. Joan was struck by Tony's sensuous grace and intellectual chic. But since her relish for the good life had survived recycling, she considered Tony's hip but no-frills countercultural life-style somewhat grubby. "I went to Broadway openings in my full-length black velvet cape," she recalls, "and Tony went in his cutoffs."

Joan balked at moving into Tony's unimpressive digs in Brooklyn Heights, but he swept her off her feet with a romantic trip to the Bahamas. It worked, but says Joan, "that was the last thing he ever showed me. From there on in, it was one continual hassle over money. I kept moving up the ladder, from assistant editor to editor to senior editor, while Tony stayed in a rut. I resented his lack of ambition. He had a terrific notion of an egalitarian two-career family, and I wanted him to get off his ass and earn more money. Forget what I was earning—I wanted *him* to support me in style."

Joan was about to move out on Tony when it occurred to her that theirs was a *territorial* problem. "I tried to imagine how it would be living with him in a different setting—in a better environment—and I could see that all we needed was a change of scene. I loved Tony; I *didn't* love living in Brooklyn Heights."

The solution was relatively simple. Joan and Tony bought a second home in Sag Harbor that satisfied Joan's need both for status and for a retreat from the urban scene. As long as it wasn't holding her back from the good life anymore, Tony's "lack of ambition" lost its sting. Joan saw him for what he was—the right man for her in all else except income.

Bear in mind, however, that contributing to the purchase of a home (or whatever else it'll take to make you feel "rich") won't always supply the missing half of the loaf with a man of limited means. You can't buy your way out of a hole if the man himself, apart from his finances, falls far short of the mark. Who he is always takes precedence over what he has or might have in different circumstances.

Always look to see whether a man's lack of earning power arises out of a changeable situation (his youth, the economy) or out of an inherent wimpishness that you can't accommodate. *And never underestimate the power of your preferences.* If you can't support a relationship without feeling exploited, don't try to pretend that you can. Flexibility about your preferences is greatly to be desired; self-deception will lead you astray.

At best, a Half-Loaf is a flawed relationship that can be improved but not corrected. You can gain handsomely from it as long as you don't allow it to restrict your other options. *Exert your power!* Resist pressure—from him, others, yourself— to make this a lasting relationship. Keep cultivating new contacts through your network, and don't feel constrained to turn down other dates.

Above all, never deplete your resources in an extravagant attempt to make a Half-Loaf more than it is. The most pitiful victims of love are those women (and men) who go profoundly into debt or drive themselves to the brink of mental collapse in order to force a marginal relationship beyond its natural life. You can avoid joining their numbers by never lying to yourself about the *quality* of an affair. That, and that alone, should determine the size of your investment in it and its possibilities for permanence.

3. *The Dress Rehearsal*

This could be it—*almost*. All along, as you've been working your way up the love ladder—from casual sex to dating to your first semipermanent relationship—you've been like an actor preparing for opening night. You've been perfecting your lines, polishing your moves, sharpening your vision of the total effect that you want to achieve. Your Dress Rehearsal is the big run-through where you hone your readiness to the max and pin down what does and does not "play." You may even discover that you need yet another cast change—namely, a new leading man. But while the right one is waiting in the wings, you're getting your act together in this Dress Rehearsal, a relationship that *could* be the real thing except that it's unfinished. It's still part of the process of *getting there*, rather than the arrival itself. Nonetheless, it's a perfect opportunity to work out the bugs in your craft and evolve a fully realized role in love in preparation for that smash hit.

Unlike the Wellington and the Half-Loaf, the Dress Rehearsal is an authentic and relatively unflawed relationship. It's destined for impermanence only because you've met each other at a time when a lasting commitment can't be given. The barriers to permanence don't arise out of a poor connection but rather from some external condition—timing, the need to relocate, the reappearance of a former love partner, a family crisis, etc.

A typical Dress Rehearsal is the "little marriage" practiced by two students who are well matched and genuinely love each other but can't remain committed permanently because life is pulling them in different directions. They're unsettled as to the most fundamental aspects of life, like career choices or where each of them will want to live. A couple like this usually breaks up when one of them graduates and moves away. Sometimes they reestablish the relationship later (remember Linda, the doctor who changed residencies to be reunited with her medical-school sweetheart?), but often they don't.

A woman in a campus Dress Rehearsal can minimize her losses by being aware at the outset of the low probability of permanence. Lori, a petite, feisty sophomore at Brown, is a good example. She wasn't looking for a boyfriend when she literally bumped into Gary as she was flying down the library

steps. (Your chances of finding someone when you're not looking are better because spontaneity catches both of you off-
guard—you're not anxious about making a good impression,
and he's not as wary of entrapment as he would be if he met
you in a more structured situation.)

Gary, a soft-spoken, sandy-haired junior, was rushing up
the stairs while Lori was hurrying down, and they collided.
As Gary apologetically helped Lori pick up her books, they
struck up a conversation that ended with a date to have dinner
that night. "It wasn't a *date* date," Lori says, "just a casual 'let's
get together tonight' kind of thing. You always make those
vague promises when you meet someone you like, but this
time we both meant it."

Over a mushroom pizza that night, they discovered that
they had a lot in common: both were nineteen-year-old (Gary
had skipped a year) journalism majors from upper-middle-class
families; both loved sports, pinball, old movies, and Agatha
Christie novels. They whiled away the night talking about
everything from Bach to Bogart films. Soon they moved beyond
dating into a warm, wonderful affair.

Lori and Gary were inseparable, whether hiking through
Europe or collaborating on a TV documentary that they hoped
to peddle to the networks. Their friends and families accepted
them as a couple. Gary spent a whole summer living with Lori
and her family in their two-bedroom Upper East Side apartment while he interned at a radio newsroom in Manhattan,
and Lori met Gary's family when he brought her home with
him during their midterm break. They were totally and avowedly
committed to each other, but permanence was not in their
plans. In fact, the very mention of it horrified them.

Because their Dress Rehearsal had all the makings of a lasting
relationship, people were puzzled by this seeming contradic-
tion. They assumed that a couple so deeply committed to one
another would want to be together the rest of their lives. But
Gary made it clear that while Lori was the only one for him

at this time in his life, he wouldn't be ready for marriage until he was in his thirties and established in his career.

Lori had no intentions of changing his mind. If anything, she was even more adamant about keeping her own options open. She remembers an incident that happened when she was sitting around the dinner table with Gary's family during the Christmas holidays. Gary's younger sister, Caroline, an East Coast Valley Girl who assumed Lori had "landed" her brother, began talking about their future: "When you guys get married—"

Lori quickly interrupted her. She didn't mean to be rude to Caroline, but thought she should set her straight. "Hey, give me a break," Lori pleaded, "I'm only nineteen. I love Gary, but I'm not getting tied down. There's a lot ahead of me. I've got to finish school, get a graduate degree, and find a good job. Please don't talk to me about marriage. God, I don't even want to think about it!"

Contrast Lori's confident management-by-objective approach to love with the self-destructiveness of the desperate husband-hunter and you can see the necessity for always dealing from a position of strength. Lori will probably get what she wants in both her career and her love life because she knows where she's coming from at every moment. She's not about to be pressured into making a premature marriage that would truncate the overall shape of her life.

The key to having it all is the ability to shift your work and love priorities without foreclosing on either one. While you're moving ahead on one front, you've still got to keep your eye on the other. But remember, your options are continuously unfolding. Don't yield to that infamous "last chance" mentality (when you're nineteen and in love, this is *not* your last chance to get married; when you're twenty-five and thinking of having a family, this is *not* your last chance to work).

The best decisions in these matters evolve out of your own gut feelings. There's no need to be defensive about them—

we're talking about choices here, not judgments. All I can say to you at this tender stage of your life is this: If your career is your first priority, it's not selfish to sacrifice a relationship for it when you can't reconcile his plans with your own. On the other hand, you're not "selling out" when you bend your career plans to accommodate someone you love. In either case, the campus Dress Rehearsal is an answer for the student who wants an internship in the world of love while she's busy carving out a career path.

If you've acknowledged that a campus Dress Rehearsal generally isn't meant to last, you can let go of it with your dignity intact. In the event that the moving finger of time should write Gary out of Lori's scenario, for example, there'll be the bittersweet feelings of loss and sadness along with loving memories, but there won't be raging anger and shock.

Another kind of Dress Rehearsal is the one that stops short of permanence because one of the partners doesn't want to have children. The baby barrier usually crops up when there's a significant disparity in ages. While the age glitch doesn't seem to matter *per se*, it can preclude a lasting relationship between an older person who doesn't want any more children and a younger one who does.

Marty, a forty-four-year-old Porsche-Audi dealer, told me about his relationship with Janet, a twenty-six-year-old hygienist. He's low-key, stylish, slight, and wiry-looking; she's a bubbly, youthfully polished blonde. Marty had been a long-time patient of Janet's boss. In the course of his conversations with her, Marty revealed that he was supporting two children from a previous marriage. His divorce had been amicable and he saw his children often.

As Marty's relationship with Janet progressed from cleaning teeth to clinging passion, they discovered that they were remarkably compatible despite their age differences. Marty asked Janet to live with him. He told her that he might want to marry her someday, but was adamant about having no more children. Janet thought it was a fair trade-off: She agreed to forgo having children, because she believed that Marty was all she'd ever need.

They moved in together and were keenly happy for the next several years. But on the brink of her thirtieth birthday, Janet began to act as if she'd made a bargain with the devil. At first only a stirring, her yearning to have a baby became increasingly deep. Obsessed with the idea of motherhood, she'd stare wistfully at toddlers on the street and talk almost constantly about how wonderful children were and how empty she felt without one of her own. Marty was up against the biological clock. "It was a no-win situation," he says, explaining why he and Janet reluctantly split. "I should have met her twenty years earlier when I was just starting out. We were a good match in everything except the phases of our lives."

If you're looking for real permanence and not a Dress Rehearsal, keep your eye on that biological clock. At a time when more and more women are putting off childbearing in favor of career-building, Janet's experience with "baby hunger" is becoming a common condition. Like a gathering ocean wave that sneaks up from behind and flattens you, "baby hunger" strikes without warning.

According to psychologist Lois Leiderman Davitz, who herself experienced this urgent need to have a child and subsequently bore a son, the intense emotional tug for babies enters your consciousness in a variety of ways. Called "peaking," they range from a sudden aversion to contraceptives to the symptoms of a false pregnancy. In her provocative article for *McCall's* magazine ("Baby Hunger," November 1981), Dr. Davitz discusses the results of a study she conducted with her psychologist husband in which a cross section of women were asked a series of questions regarding life-style and children.

"Not one woman reacted mildly or dismissed the [issue] as irrelevant," she reports. "Many women today are more comfortable with the notion that having a baby is an individual's choice and that a desire to have a child is a result of conditioning rather than an emotional drive. Our study, though, suggests that this assumption just isn't true. Whether it occurs at 28 or 38, whether it is somewhat powerful or virtually overwhelming, the desire, when it comes, is backed by an emotional intensity that cannot be attributed to social or cultural stereotypes alone." You're sure of your life—sure of your job—when you begin to feel that there *must* be more to life than work. Your orderly world is thrown into turmoil when you try to fight or (much worse) ignore those conflicting inner urges.

When you're in your twenties, the jury is still out on the basic, biological issue of childbearing. Postponement shouldn't be confused with safely writing it off once and for all. You can't predict how you'll feel years in the future when your internal clock ticks down to your zero hour: the day when you can no longer become pregnant. At that time, you may (or may not) fall prey to "baby hunger."

When someone is through with or opposed to having children, that's a different story. Now you're into the finality of an irrevocable decision. Don't minimize it! A variance here doesn't have the same flexibility as the glitch between a partygoer vs. a homebody, or a rugged outdoorsman vs. a pampered princess. While life-style differences may be tough to negotiate, the baby barrier, regardless of which side of it you're on, is an insuperable bar to permanence.

By way of encouragement, let me point out that the urge for biological parenthood can sometimes be satisfied vicariously through what is commonly known as a "ready-made" family. Rita, a divorced forty-year-old travel agent with two teen-age children, was fully prepared to have nothing more than a Dress Rehearsal with Doug, the personable young stockbroker who befriended her when she arranged a business trip for him to Cancún. Rita was wary because she didn't want to be tied down with young kids again while Doug, never-married at thirty-five, hadn't fathered any. But, happily, the baby barrier that Rita anticipated never arose. Says Rita, now married to Doug, "Most of us aren't that selfless about parenthood. But Doug is that rare man who doesn't feel the need to reproduce himself. He relates to my children as if they were his."

Rita was lucky, but don't forget that she was also smart. She was aware of the *potential* for trouble and therefore wouldn't have been devastated had it materialized. The implicit danger in a Dress Rehearsal is its insidious resemblance to the real thing. You can easily get so caught up in the Dress Rehearsal's illusion of long-term validity that you can't see the forces lying in wait to bring it down. When the breakup comes, it catches you off-guard and overwhelms you with its element of *predictable surprise* (you should have seen it coming).

My friend Randi, now joyously married, had a traumatic Dress Rehearsal that was the capstone of her single days and a vivid example of the shock value of predictable surprise. Randi, a talented fashion photographer in her forties, had been out of her marriage to an affluent, country-clubbing dentist for about four years when she met Dan. Initially, Randi discounted Dan for a serious relationship because his Bible Belt working-class background clashed with her northeastern moneyed sophistication, and his craggy weather-beaten look was offensive to a woman who preferred middle-aged preppies. But as the editor and publisher of a graphic-arts magazine, Dan shared Randi's creative sensibilities more fully than any man she'd ever known.

"People couldn't contain their surprise when I showed up at parties with this hulking, overgrown hayseed," Randi says. "On the surface we certainly weren't well matched, but privately it worked. We loved to exchange ideas and observations. Sex was very primitive and powerful. Dan was a selfless lover—almost *too* selfless. He had a weak ego and a constant need for approval and admiration in everything he did. I was a mirror of his greatness, you might say, but I could deal with it because I saw that same side of him in myself."

Randi admits that her relationship with Dan had some of the conscious compromise of a Half-Loaf ("I knew I was set-tling"), but she also admits that a certain failure of will might have lured her into marrying him eventually. "When you're tired of the searching, exclusivity becomes very seductive," she explains. "You get hooked on the absence of risk. Dan was a family man who hated the single life as much as I did. He hustled me into an exclusive relationship before I knew what was happening. Then the momentum started to build, and marriage seemed like the inevitable next step."

If Randi had been paying attention, she'd have known that Dan already *was* married in a sense—divorced from his wife, but not separated. He talked about Lee, his ex-wife, often enough for Randi to get the picture. A flight attendant who'd given up her job for marriage, Lee was still living in domestic misery with their three children—Beth, Matthew, and four-year-old Ricky—in a hick town in upstate New York. The divorce had been Lee's idea. She wanted to be free to go back to school and on to a new life, and she was counting on good old reliable Dan to help her out with the kids while she was shifting gears. But Dan surprised her. Instead of staying put as a struggling instructor at the local community college, he seized on their separation as *his* chance to start over. He moved to Manhattan, got an M.B.A. at Columbia, and jockeyed him-self into a glamorous and high-paying job.

It was hard for Dan not to gloat as reports of his success drifted back to Lee through the gossip mill. He knew that Lee was jealous, and he took a queer satisfaction in her retaliation through custody battles and guilt trips over the kids. "They were playing some kind of sick game," Randi says. "All these irate letters flying back and forth all the time. I knew there was more than the normal unfinished business between them, but I blocked it out. They'd been apart for over four years, and after all that time I didn't see Lee as any real threat."

Randi was dumb, dumb, dumb! *Every* ex-wife (or former lover) is a real threat until she's safely married. It's the *finality* of the break that determines a man's freedom from a previous relationship, not the length of time that's elapsed since the break occurred.

How can you judge the finality of a break? Certainly not by what a man tells you about its being over, nor even by how he acts toward you. That was Randi's mistake. She assumed that because she had the upper hand in her relationship with Dan, she could trust him implicitly in all things. But a man's willingness to please is not to be confused with undying devotion. If *you're* calling the shots with him, so did the woman who was there before you. And should it come to a showdown between you and her, since she preceded you in time (and has a stronger hold on him through the kids, the in-laws, the family dog, et al.), she has first dibs. In short, never count out a predecessor unless she *is* out for good.

In retrospect, Randi acknowleges that she had every reason to suspect the worst where Lee was concerned. The woman simply wouldn't let go. "Her letters were like pages out of a textbook on how to produce guilt," Randi says. "When a particularly bad one came, Dan would show it to me in disbelief. Once she wrote, 'Your son Matthew was so excited when he saw your name mentioned in *Newsweek*. He still idolizes you and doesn't hold it against you for turning your back on your family to seek the recognition you always craved.' Another time she went on and on about the problems the boys were having growing up without a father. She ended that one with 'It broke my heart today when I bumped into your friend Leon in the mall and little Ricky ran up to him and asked, 'Are you my daddy?' "

Besides the letters, there were the telephone calls that came with depressing regularity. Randi would sit by helplessly while Dan and Lee wrangled heatedly over visitation rights. "Occasionally, I'd overhear Lee screaming into the receiver like a shrew," Randi says, "and I couldn't imagine how Dan was ever married to her, let alone that he'd want to go back." But Randi was simply ignoring the evidence. The loss of Lee bothered Dan almost as much as the absence of his children. His divorce was still a touchy subject. Discussing it with Randi, his objectivity would often dissolve into anguish, and he'd blurt out things like "How could a woman turn her back on a fifteen-year marriage just like *that?*"

Part of the problem, Randi realizes now, is that she wasn't willing to go the extra mile to become a genuine replacement for Lee. "I was terribly caught up in a work project when I met Dan," she says, "and I wouldn't put myself out for him if it interfered with my plans. I think that scared him. He balked whenever I mentioned marriage. He talked a liberated game, but at heart what he wanted was a traditional housewife. I wanted a two-career marriage with a lot of personal freedom and very few domestic demands. Marrying him would have been a disaster, but I kept pushing for marriage anyway. He was right to be skeptical. I was thinking about my immediate security, not what life together would be like in the long run."

In the year that they went together, Randi saw Dan's children only once. After months of battling with Lee over the terms, Dan arranged a visit with the kids at Christmas. His car piled with decoratively wrapped gifts and a little folding aluminum tree with all the trimmings, Dan drove Randi up to the town near Albany where his family lived. They checked into a motel, put up the tree and arranged the gifts, and had a wonderful night of lovemaking.

"The next morning, we got up early," Randi recalls. "Dan went to get the kids, and I went out for the pretzels and the potato chips. We had a great little party, very special in its own way. Dan's kids were likable and well behaved. I was touched by their affection. Ricky climbed into my lap and hugged me for getting him the video game he'd wanted, and on the way back to their house after lunch, Beth insisted on stopping and buying me flowers with her own money. I know it was an idealized situation, but it made me think that Dan and I and his kids could all be happy together."

Cut to three months later on a Friday night at eight o'clock. Randi was waiting for Dan to pick her up for their standing weekend date. This weekend was especially important because Dan was leaving on a business trip to Florida that coming Monday and wouldn't be back for two weeks. "Dan was late, and it wasn't like him not to call," Randi remembers. "By nine o'clock, I was really worried. I called his place. No answer. I tried to track him down through friends we knew. Still no luck. I started to imagine the worst—an accident, a heart attack, God knows what."

Beside herself, Randi went over to Dan's apartment to see what had happened. "Everything looked fine," she says. "The place was neat as a pin; the phone worked. His bags were standing near the kitchen, so I knew he hadn't been called away early. I went into the den and began riffling through the papers on his desk for some clue. Suddenly, I spotted my name on a sheet of paper. It was a long, typewritten letter. I picked it up and started reading. Midway into the first paragraph, I went into shock. My heart was roaring in my ears, and I felt like the victim of a brutal assault."

The letter read:

> My dearest Randi,
> I want to thank you for giving me one of the most memorable years of my life. You're the brightest, most exciting and sensuous woman a man could ever hope to find. I'll always be grateful for the many special times we shared. Please believe that I care for you deeply and don't want to cause you pain. However, for a long time there's been

a sadness in my life that even you couldn't make me forget. Now, at last, I've found what was missing—the love that no one else but Lee can give me.

Three weeks ago, while you were on assignment in Houston, Lee wrote me the most reaching out letter I've ever read. In it, she told me she'd made a terrible mistake and begged me to forgive her. She asked me to give our marriage another try. Her letter hit home like none of the others. It made me see in black and white how badly I was jeopardizing my children's future by living apart from them during this formative time in their lives.

I drove up to see Lee to talk things over. We talked for hours on end, and feelings that had been buried for years came tumbling out. Tearfully, we started to embrace. The children realized what was happening and came running into the room. Soon we were all laughing and crying at the same time. Later that night after the kids were asleep, Lee led me into the bedroom we had shared for fifteen years. Trembling with desire, we fell into our old bed and made love.

I know you will understand how important it is for me to be united with my family. The time you and I had together is precious to me, and I'll treasure it forever. I sincerely hope that we can remain loving friends. I'll always be in your corner.

Love,
Dan

Randi read the letter over and over again, each time with growing anger. She thought, You dirty son of a bitch, how dare you! How could you sneak behind my back like that and not have the decency to tell me face-to-face what happened? Only a cowardly creep would send a hokey "Dear Jane" letter. And then it hit her: *This is a Xerox.*

"The bastard had it all figured out," says Randi. "The original was in the mail to me. If I hadn't been smart enough to find the copy, I wouldn't have been reading the letter until Monday, when Dan was safely away in Florida with no way for me to reach him for *two whole weeks*. I wanted to kill him! He thought I'd get over him in two weeks' time and would quietly fade into the past. He wanted to avoid a scene."

But the scene was not to be avoided. Randi knew that Dan would have to come home to get his bags, and she decided to wait for him even if it meant sitting up all night. Shortly after midnight he walked into his apartment, and Randi accosted him, angrily waving his letter in her hand. She demanded to know where he'd been and he said simply, "With her."

At that, Randi flew into a rage. "I completely lost control," she says. "I screamed obscenities at him and threw a candy dish against the wall. It was like *Virginia Woolf*. At one point, I ran into the kitchen with his letter, ripped it to shreds, and threw it in the garbage. I picked up a bread knife and would've killed him with it if he hadn't stopped me. I kept alternating between hating his guts and wanting to throw myself at him and seduce him into coming back."

When she calmed down, Dan tried to explain that he hadn't left her for another woman—it was his *family* that had won out over her. She stared miserably at him, thinking about the nice, warm fold he was returning to while she was being dumped unceremoniously out in the cold. She despised the smug look on Dan's face—the same peculiar mix of sympathy and triumph that was in his letter. Suddenly she understood that he wanted this reconciliation more than anything in the world, had wanted it all along. More than Dan's deception, it was her own lack of awareness that had led her to this humiliating pass. Summoning what was left of her dignity, Randi walked out and never saw Dan again.

Six months later Randi met her current husband, a Blue Ribbon type who is infinitely classier and more suitable for her than Dan. "I didn't know it then," she says, "but Lee did me the biggest favor by taking Dan back. She also taught me a good lesson—never to let ignorance be your guide in a relationship. Contrary to what people say, it's what you *don't* know that hurts you. I don't think you should stay completely in the dark about a man's life and rely on him to keep you from getting hurt. It's up to you to protect your own interests by being alert to what's really going on."

Live and learn, m'dear—that's what the semipermanent relationship is all about. After any of them ends—the Wellington, the Half-Loaf, the Dress Rehearsal, or some combination thereof (the varieties are numberless)—you're apt to feel depressed. If, like Randi, you've paid too little attention to the downside risk, you may even feel outraged enough to scream, "I'll *never* trust a man again!" (Those, by the way, were Randi's exact words to me the day after Dan jilted her.) Don't underestimate your recuperative powers. You *will* trust a man again, only you'll be a little smarter about it the next time around. You'll be less likely to trust without reservation when you should be dealing at arm's length.

If you're marriage-minded, banish the thought that a semipermanent relationship has wasted your time. Don't forget that the criterion is always how much you've grown in power and ability. Think how in each case you learned something that could prevent you from making the same mistake ever again. With the Wellington, you learned not to fake or be faked out by the appearance of the real thing. With the Half-Loaf, you learned not to try to compromise your most cherished priorities. And with the Dress Rehearsal, you learned not to ignore certain external barriers to love that stand in the way of permanence.

More than that, as we'll see, it's these semipermanents that will lead you to the Right One by helping you to define ever more clearly who that is.

The very act of sustaining a relationship, even if it ends disappointingly, increases your chances for ultimate success by strengthening your confidence and skills. No one is born an expert in the art of loving; we all have to learn through the trial-and-error process. You may choose to bypass the Wellington and Half-Loaf if they're inherently repellent to you, but be prepared to have any number of Dress Rehearsals before you're ready for lasting love.

Curiously enough, when you look back on your semipermanent relationships, you'll rejoice that they were only *semi* and not permanent. Love is Darwinian: Only the fittest attachments survive. Like the dinosaur, your near-misses were nature's rejects. They didn't hold up under the test of time, because something better was on the way.

MORAL: The one that got away did you a favor.

7

The Right One

*R*are is the woman who achieves success in love today without having loved different men in different ways at different times in her life. But that doesn't mean that the concept of the Right One—or Right Ones—is a myth. Like success in work, success in love requires *focus*. To reach the top of the love ladder, you have to know where the top is and how to get there. Out of all the possible men you could love, you must narrow your sights down to a particular type of man who represents the best match for you in terms of two things: *attraction* and *compatibility*.

Just as surely as there's a right job for you, there's a right man. Consider the work world for a moment. Isn't it absurd to think you could be happy and successful in *any* line of work—from carving tombstones to splicing genes—if only you tried hard enough? You know yourself well enough to understand that you can't will monuments or designer genes to be your thing, and yet you may not be able to rule them out conclusively until you try your hand at them.

It's the same with men, except that they're infinitely more various than jobs and call for a more complicated trial-and-error process. It's a process that entails going through many different experiences—schoolgirl crushes, flirtations, dates, sexual flings, relationships—before certain common denominators conducive to success or failure can be seen.

At this point in the love game, you should be able to discern basic similarities in the men you find most attractive or the ones you get along with best. Attraction, you realize to your sorrow, doesn't always go hand in hand with compatibility. But the more you learn about attraction and compatibility as they play out in your own life, the better able you are to piece together a profile of the man with whom you'll be most likely to succeed in love by having both. That man—and you may find him more than once in a lifetime—is the Right One.

Many women have an aversion to being clearheaded about love; they think that objectivity diminishes romantic excitement. But the ultimate, most breathtaking excitement in love comes from linking up with someone who *fits*, and instinct alone usually isn't enough to guide you toward that person. You need criteria. Without a working knowledge of those qualities that make a man a good choice for you (you've already learned the ones that certify disaster), you may never get beyond a semipermanent relationship to lasting love.

The idea that you *fall* rather than *choose* to be in love stems from that archaic notion of women's helplessness. It was the man who did the choosing; the woman concentrated on getting chosen. It's astonishing how little that has changed today. Despite the fact that women are now exercising their right of choice in every other aspect of their lives, in love they're still operating on the old assumption that "it's a man's world." They're either waiting to be discovered by the Right One (whoever that is) or they're taking up indiscriminately with Everyman on the slim chance that he may turn out to be right. Most women haven't learned to approach love the way men do— as a matter up for decision. Men look for love; women hope for it.

The secret of finding the Right One is to know who that is. Realistic selectivity is the key. The reason you find love when you're *ready* to find it is that you've finally learned how to manage your objectives. You've formulated a well-developed image of an attractive and compatible partner, and you've made a conscious decision to seek that person out and establish a satisfying relationship with him.

Let's consider what occurs when a man tires of the single life and gets ready to settle down. I've seen this happen so often that I know it's no accident: When there's no percentage for him anymore in picking losers, his luck suddenly improves. Why? Because he's motivated. He has knocked around long enough to know that he wants to be committed to a particular kind of woman, and now he's going after her with an undivided sense of purpose.

Look how he changes his moves. Instead of discarding his current love because she has only eighty-four attributes out of his checklist of eighty-five (he started with ten), our heretofore confirmed bachelor begins to think that maybe eighty-four are enough. Or he relocates from Alaska, where the only available women are Eskimos, and adopts a life-style more likely to attract the sophisticated type of woman he wants. Or he stops chasing after inaccessible women who can't commit to him because they're married or neurotic or want someone else, and he starts paying attention to the one who really cares. What's he doing? *He's taking control of the possibilities for success.* By eliminating the wrong ones—a goddess, an Eskimo, a manipulator—he's homing in closer and closer on the one who could be right.

Men who are seriously looking for a partner have an enviable capacity to reel off the specifications a woman must meet to satisfy their individual needs. They usually arrive at these specs by making mistakes as dumb as ours (we're in this together), but men learn from their errors better than we do because they have more confidence in their right not to repeat them.

Let me give you an example. Ted, a divorced man I know, spent a year or so of "wasted nights" romancing young space cadets before his ex-wife's speedy remarriage gave him the impetus for a midcourse correction. Without that galvanic event, his run of bad luck might have continued indefinitely. But with the sudden urge to get on with his life and marry again, too, Ted realized that a twenty-year-old flash dancer wasn't for him.

After giving it some thought, Ted knew that what he wanted, in contrast to what he'd been getting, was a mature companion with school-age kids who could help him reconstruct the family setting he missed so much. When he talked to me about finding the Right One, he was able to articulate this longing with an honest wisdom that went well beyond the "attractive, classy, bright Sagittarius" jargon of the personal ads. Once he redirected his search for a good partner, it didn't take him long to find her.

Men's belief in their prerogative to choose a partner is one that we should emulate. Because we're unfamiliar with the power of choice in love, our specifications for a partner are usually unformed or, if formed, are the stuff of romantic fantasy rather than real life. Either we want a domesticated Gorgeous Brute—a man who exudes the self-confidence of the masterful hero in Gothic novels but who, unlike that powerful father figure, doesn't make all the decisions, subdue us with physical force, and insist that he's always right, or we want Mr. Sensitivity, that marvel of emotional openness who never bares his insecurities or self-doubts and never defers to us about what movie to see or where to eat lest we accuse him of being a wimp.

Not only are we cripplingly vague or unrealistic about our preferences, we're often defensive about them, too. If we don't feel so guilty about wanting a man who meets our legitimate requirements that we dispense with our standards altogether, then we go in the opposite direction and freak out on perfection, using our criteria as a shield against ever giving anyone who *almost* measures up an even break.

Career-oriented "superstars" are the worst offenders in the perfectionist class. You know who you are—'fess up. We're tired of hearing you bitch and moan about the shortage of available men out there when you make it harder for yourself with your uncompromising attitude. You want success in love without tears or sweat. Well, she who's looking for a free lunch goes hungry—love's not for whiners.

Here's the answer. Let your absorption in the challenge crowd out those depressing thoughts of drudgery, and your search for the Right One will become even more captivating than the hustle for a career payoff. Besides, the alternatives stink. Being alone, like hooking up with a married mentor who knows and loves you exactly as you are but only on Thursday nights, never leads to anything but more of the same.

Having dispensed with the preliminaries, we'll now undertake the main work of mapping out a mental diagram of the man who's right for you—one whose configuration of inner and outer qualities is most likely to fit in well with your own. To help you form a picture of this man that's clear enough to guide you to him, here are some of my observations and pet theories about the nature of attraction and compatibility.

Surfaces and Centers

When you reexamine your pattern in love, you'll find that attraction is governed by the surfaces we present to each other, and compatibility by how we connect at our centers. While we're often attracted to someone dissimilar to us in outward style, his inner self must be in agreement with ours for a good connection. Opposites may attract, but it's likes who pair up most successfully.

Let's suppose that you're a vivacious, dynamic spitfire on the surface and you're frequently drawn to the strong silent type whose style is more logical, controlled, and goal-oriented. You're attracted to each other because you both see your two contrasting styles—the emotional vs. the mental—as complementary: His outward style has precisely those characteristics of control and cool-headedness that you'd like to have in yourself; and he, feeling inhibited by his own reserve and lack of spontaneity, gravitates toward you because he thinks you're warm, loving, vital, and fun.

If you go on to establish a good relationship with him, both of you can take advantage of these surface differences. You can learn from each other, share strengths, compensate for inadequacies, and expand your lives. But that won't happen unless the centers of yourselves—and I'm defining the *center* as the core of needs and beliefs underlying each person's outward style—are in basic agreement. You must either share the same world view and want the same things out of life or share the same degree of mental health (or mental disturbance) so that being together satisfies your deepest desires.

When your centers are out of sync, no matter how attracted you are to each other, being together can be about as satisfying as a terminal illness. For example, let's say that your dynamic outward style makes him see you as the perfect partner—an aggressive, passionate woman who'll liven up his life without invading his cherished privacy. But he could be in for a surprise. Like someone biting into a piece of chocolate for a Brazil nut and finding a soft center instead, he may discover, beneath the inviting glow of your surface warmth, not the independence he expected but a need to be coddled and reassured.

You could be in for a surprise, too. What you don't know—and have to find out—is whether he's really as strong and supportive inside as his cool, calm surface implies. Provided that your need for nurturance isn't excessive or incessant, you have a right to have it satisfied. The question is, Is what you need from him consistent with what he thinks he should be asked to give?

If your centers are such that you clash on this very fundamental issue of emotional roles—you want a nurturer, and he thinks you're hanging on him to be fed—you're in big trouble. Instead of achieving that ideal collaboration you hoped to bring about between your contrasting outward styles—making his dispassionate, mental approach to life more human and your feisty, emotional approach more mellow—you get polarized in opposite directions. You become an overemotional shrew who's always laying your feelings on him and demanding to know how he feels. And to protect his feelings, he becomes exaggeratedly rational and constantly fends you off with non-committal replies. Because your centers don't fit, your attractive surface differences are like concealed weapons.

Disagreement on emotional roles is one glitch at the center that may not come to light right away. Only the worst cases are apparent. For example, it doesn't take long to figure out that a man who goes brain-dead when you confide your worries to him (but who keeps you up half the night listening to his) isn't a born nurturer. Even so, you may be so attracted to this oaf as to think you can negotiate your need for nurturance by disciplining yourself to ask for less and training him to give more. Theoretically, this should be possible, but such negotiation demands a more flexible center than most people have.

It stands to reason that by widening your range, *healthy flexibility* increases your chances for success in love. I say "healthy" because flexibility is an advantage only when it's based on a sense of personal power. It's a form of generosity, not submissiveness: You're giving *to* the other person, not giving *in*.

Healthy flexibility sets an inspiring example for a man: Women who don't always have to have their way usually get it. They get it by putting a cap on their demands and by showing appreciation for what's given. (Appreciation, by the way, almost makes a cap unnecessary. It's the ultimate incentive in a relationship because a man who likes to please will do practically anything for a woman, short of homicide, as long as she gives him glowing performance reports.) A healthily flexible woman, then, is one who'll *moderate* her demands on a man but won't disavow them and try to change her soft center into a Brazil nut in order to accommodate him.

In contrast to healthy flexibility, there's something I call the "chameleon complex"—a form of subservience rather than adaptability. It stems from a feeling of powerlessness in relationships that makes you abdicate your right to choose someone whose center roughly coincides with yours. You abandon selectivity and, like the women stuck in Half-Loaves, try to make the Right One out of whoever comes your way. Ignoring even the most serious glitch, you struggle to bring your incongruous center into conformity with his—and you fail.

The thing to remember about love is that a certain amount of *natural* compatibility is a given. Being healthily flexible can reduce the amount of natural compatibility that you need, but it can't do away with it altogether. Experts in the art of selling have uncovered a powerful law of human motivation that determines *every* choice we make, from the purchase of a product to the selection of a spouse: *We like people who are like ourselves.* In love, a corollary to that law might be: *Happiness is finding your romantic twin.*

I know what you're thinking: It's hard enough finding *a man,* let alone complicating the search by looking for your romantic twin. Everybody has probably told you that if you weren't so particular you'd be married by now, and I'm telling you to be yet more particular—hardly what you want to hear. But the fact is that by narrowing your search to your male twin—a man who shares similar traits and agrees with you on the fundamental issues—you'll shorten your looking time and improve your chances of romantic success.

When you take the position that you have the right to choose a man who doesn't require bending your center out of shape to fit his, as the "chameleon complex" dictates, you avoid getting drawn into one impossible incompatibility after another. Having a model of a man *based on your own objectives* cuts down the likelihood of overcommitting yourself to an irredeemable mismatch and helps steer you toward a relationship imbued with that vital element of natural compatibility.

Contrary to the Puritan belief that anything effortless is the work of the devil, I've found that relationships "made in heaven" are the ones that require very little work. There seems to be a definite correlation between the quality of the relationship and the level of effortlessness: The better the relationship, the less you have to work at it. This might be so because both people have done a lot of work on themselves individually, but I think that a high degree of natural compatibility is a big factor.

I don't mean to imply that if you have to work at a relationship, it can't work. Even the most heavenly match is often spiced with a little conflict, and the lack of it could signal the plastic perfection of a Wellington rather than bliss. Your romantic twin doesn't have to be your clone (how narcissistic can you get?). He can be markedly different from you in outward style or have other surface disagreements and still be an ideal companion. But when it comes to your deeply held priorities, unless you're exceedingly flexible (or he is), the Right One should be like your mirror image—a man who complements you so beautifully or has so much in common with you that a bond exists of its own accord.

Once you've got your network in place and have gone through enough preparatory relationships, you'll begin to realize that your romantic twin is not as difficult to find as you once thought. He's like any other close and trusted friend you've made in your life except that he's dynamite in bed—he's a male friend who's caught fire. Like your best friend (or business partner), he's someone with whom you have that all-important "meeting of the minds": Your perceptions have the same frame of reference; you speak the same language of the heart; you share secrets without feeling judged; you have similar opinions of other people; you find the same things funny.

It's this "meeting of the minds" that enables some couples who are outwardly very different—a staid conservative vs. a feisty liberal, or a fitness freak vs. someone whose idea of exercise is a loud yawn—to be deliciously compatible with each other. Their agreement on what's important to them as a couple neutralizes differences that are less important. How far apart two people are politically or athletically isn't critical if those priorities are superseded by the ones that are shared— let's say, emotional closeness, sex, social activity, family life, intellectual interests, standard of living, etc. A compatible partner is someone you don't have to make over in your own image, because he's already *in* your image in all the ways that count.

On All Fours

By now you've learned a basic law of attraction and compatibility: You can't *fake* attraction, and you can't *make* compatibility. You have to be honest with *yourself* about the first, and honest with *him* about the other.

While attraction is a necessity for success in love, it's a totally unreliable predictor of it; only high marks in compatibility can tell you whether you'll be happy with a man you think is the Right One. You can tell how high you score in compatibility by testing out how well you mesh with this man on those priorities most important to each of you—and that takes knowledge, skill, and guts.

First, the knowledge. There's a saying in the legal profession that two cases are perfectly analogous if they match up "on all fours"—meaning that one set of facts fits the other right on in all relevant respects. In love, I'd say that being "on all fours" in a relationship is an apt expression, too, especially because I think you'll find it helpful to look at four major areas of priorities that have to be addressed. A conflict on any *single priority* within the four may not throw the case out, depending on how important that particular priority is to each of you. But if you're predominantly incompatible in any *whole area*, I wouldn't call him the Right One.

Looking back on your past relationships and on the ones described in the preceding chapter, you can see how priorities in love fall into these four areas of compatibility: (1) sexual, (2) personality, (3) role, (4) life-style.

Sexual Compatibility. Remember Marla, the elegant Westwood account executive of chapter 6, and her ill-fated Half-Loaf with a man who reminded her of Godzilla in a leisure suit? Despite his sexual proficiency and a new personal package, he remained as physically unsatisfying to Marla as a megavitamin taken in place of a gourmet meal.

To most people, sexual attractiveness is important. Each of us defines it differently—he may look like the Elephant Man to someone else, but *you* find him sexually attractive because he reminds you of someone you once knew, or he's like no one you've ever known. Maybe it's his style or charisma that turns you on. Who can say? The one thing I can say about sexual attractiveness is that, unless you're looking for a purely companionate arrangement, he'd better have it.

Beyond those immediate turn-on qualities that account for physical attraction, there's a much deeper force at work that's necessary for sexual compatibility. The sexual part of your center—your need for sex and your attitude toward it—must be in agreement with his. If you have a low sex drive, a long-term relationship with a man whose drive is high is like being closeted interminably with a jackhammer. The reverse is worse: Very few dilemmas in life are more frustrating, if not downright demeaning, than to have a high sex drive and be stuck with a man who couldn't care less. Without intensive and costly sex therapy, raising the drive of a profoundly indifferent man is about as easy as teaching a bear to fly.

You can be fooled occasionally by a man who's restrained

or unrestrained during courtship and then does a turnabout after he gets you, but that's only if you want to be fooled. There are many more ways to gauge a man's feelings about sex besides his behavior in bed (although that's a good one). His level of interest in sex, what he says about it, the importance he attaches to it, his general sensuousness in other areas of his life—all of these are indications of his sexuality that should be considered along with his physical expression of it.

As for the physical expression itself, techniques and skillfulness can be learned, but the *character* of a person's sexual expression isn't subject to change. Whatever that character is—controlling, greedy, selfless, reserved, forceful—it colors lovemaking with that person and is ultimately responsible for the depth of sexual satisfaction you both derive in your relationship.

To be sexually compatible with a man, neither one of you should have to be out of character with the other. For example, if you're a greedy lover who's wildly responsive, you couldn't do better than to find a daringly selfless lover whose greatest source of satisfaction is giving a woman pleasure. You might also connect well with a man whose sexual expression has a different character—let's say controlling or reserved—but the magic won't be there. No matter how empathic or technically good he is, you'll feel obliged to step out of character and inhibit your response because of his need to control or hold back.

It might seem like nit-picking to you to be concerned about the "character" of a man's sexual response when you're grateful enough to find one who's not impotent or into whips and chains. But sexual behavior can be looked upon as a kind of symbolic language of the heart—the physical translation of each person's definition of *love*. If there's something disturbing or frustrating about the whole tenor of your sexual relations with him—he's too manipulative, too distant, too tame, too demanding—that's probably a sign that you're not comple-mentary in other ways.

Don't presume that you can negotiate sexual compatibility simply by taking Fellatio I or sending him to cunnilingus class. I'm not unmindful of the advantages you can gain from de-veloping your sexual skills to the utmost, ranging all the way from becoming a better person to acquiring a killing edge over the competition. But I must warn you of the dangers of *sexual camouflage*—covering up the gaps in a relationship with tricks you learned from *Debbie Does Dallas*. That's a misuse of your talents. Use your sexual proficiency instead to express the kind of person you are as fully and honestly as possible and to help him do the same. The resulting collaboration will give you some important insights into the real meaning of your rela-tionship.

Being good in bed, like having an attractive personal pack-age, is an indispensable asset to the woman who wants to succeed in love. While the value you place on sex is an inherent priority, low as well as high, there's no justification for inep-titude. Your drive may be beyond your control, but your skills aren't. Ignorance is a dreadful handicap—you can't commu-nicate effectively through sex if you haven't mastered the basic vocabulary. Expand your repertoire! Read, practice, experi-ment. When you find the Right One, one of the most telling ways you can let him know he's right is by what you say to him sexually.

Personality Compatibility. More than anything else, the bond that exists between you and the Right One arises out of the compatibility of your personalities. I'm of the opinion that personality compatibility is the chicken that comes first and lays the egg of sexual compatibility (forgive me for that, but I couldn't resist). What I mean is that sex might or might not be good with someone whose personality isn't compatible with yours, but it's *especially* good with someone whose personality is. Why? Because that someone—the Right One—invites you to be your natural self in *all* things, not just sex.

We've already touched on one aspect of a good personality fit—complementary emotional roles. That's my "Brazil nut vs. soft center" example wherein one person's demand for softness or toughness in the other person is equal to the softness or toughness found.

Another, more familiar way of expressing this same concept is in terms of givers and takers—a taker being someone who mainly inhabits the demand side of life, and a giver being someone who's more often on the supply side. Despite our best efforts to strike a balance in ourselves between giving and taking emotionally, most of us have prevailing tendencies in one direction or the other. It's a wise woman who acknowledges these tendencies in herself and looks for them to be complemented. The best combinations are giver-taker and giver-giver. Two takers are usually an abomination.

Besides enjoying an apt balance of emotional trade with you, the Right One is tuned in to all those other facets of your personality that make you distinctly *you*—your social and cultural background, your interests, your religion, your ethnic identity, your values, your work, your family life, your temperament, your sense of fun. I'm not saying that he has to share all of these identically—he'd have to *be* you to do that—but he has to be *empathic* toward them. He can't reject them, be indifferent to them, or tolerate them with clenched teeth; he has to understand them appreciatively. And you have to do the same for him.

When I was out in the singles world, it used to annoy the hell out of me that I had to get into the orbit of each man I was dating—familiarize myself with his own little personal world. But then I began to realize that orbiting with a man was a nuisance only when I wasn't compatible with him; when we were compatible, I enjoyed being in his orbit, because it enlarged my own little personal world without making me feel uncomfortable.

Every happily married woman I've ever known has described her husband as her best friend. What makes a good friend? How do you choose one? Look around and you'll see that most people's closest friends are individuals who, as I've said before, are very much like themselves—they're from the same social and cultural sphere or share common interests.

You'll also see that many married couples—and this is the original "Schnall theory of couple resemblance"—actually *look alike*, despite differences in height or weight, because they convey deep-seated likenesses in their personalities through their outward appearance, mien, and deportment. The usual explanation for this phenomenon is that after they've lived together awhile, couples start to look alike because they've adopted each other's mannerisms out of habit. I admit this mimicking adds to couple resemblance, but I'm convinced that it's the partners' inner likenesses reflected externally that brought them together in the first place.

Maybe the two of you belong to that rapidly growing minority who can bridge widely divergent personal worlds— different religious or ethnic backgrounds, different social classes, different value systems, etc. It's happening more and more, but what makes it work is the strength of those personality priorities that *are* shared—anything from a dandy match (as in the case of Harriet and Jim in chapter 6) to the same love of art or music. He's the Right One only when your shared priorities are compelling enough to override the lack of commonality.

Life-Style Compatibility. *Life-style* is a synonym for how each person describes a five-star Saturday night. To a counterculturalist, it could mean dining on tofu burgers, going to a rock concert, getting stoned, and having group sex. To a conspicuous consumer, it could mean dressing up in a new Adolfo, being seen in an orchestra seat at the hit play *La Cage aux Folles*, and being seen having supper later at Café des Artistes. To a homebody, it could mean eating Friday night's leftovers with some jug wine and a couple of beers, watching TV all night, and falling asleep in front of the set. And so on down the list.

A person's chosen life-style involves much more than *style* alone. Money is deeply tied in with it—not simply the possession of money, but powerful beliefs about how it should be spent. Some very wealthy people have insisted, to the immense frustration of the partners who couldn't hack it with them, on having a homebody life-style that someone with a need for more excitement would find dull and confining.

A person's professional status doesn't always dictate the life-style that you might think appropriate. There are doctors who choose to live like longshoremen, and longshoremen (usually union officials) who live like doctors. What you have to determine is whether a particular man, regardless of his occupation, is amenable to the life-style *you* prefer (and how much, incidentally, you want to kick in to support it).

Take everything into consideration—how often you like to go out, where you like to go, the people you like to be with, the kind of home you like to live in, etc.—and see how those priorities agree with his. Don't think you're being picayune if something really matters to you. A "little" thing like his aversion to eating out in restaurants can be deadly if you need to eat out three nights a week for survival. Offering to pay your share won't solve your long-term problem with this man, because home cooking represents mother's milk to him, and spending money on a restaurant meal—even your money—is a sacrilege. As much as your life-style calls for eating out, that's how much his calls for eating in.

Yes, I know all those marvelous stories about the arrangements enterprising couples have worked out to negotiate their life-style differences: She's gone dancing with a girlfriend every

Saturday night for forty-five years while he's sat home dusting his rifle collection, and they're still madly in love. But you have to ask yourself if you want to live that way. You also have to ask yourself if he's capable of giving you that much freedom without feeling neglected, and vice versa.

I know that separate interests and activities can enliven a relationship, but not when you're off doing your thing to the extent that you're leading a parallel existence. Having a big enough common ground and a "meeting of the minds" on a life-style that permits enormous gobs of privacy makes the difference. The best relationships I know of today are those in which "space" is a high priority for both people, and the worst are those in which it's a high priority for *one*. You get the message: *Freedom* is another word for *discontent* when you're not in agreement on it.

Role Compatibility. Someone once made the point that if businesses failed at the rate that marriages do, we'd all be living in the forest off wild berries and the bark of trees. A big advantage business partners have over love partners is that people who are working together for a profit have a division of labor that makes sense. They each do what they excel at and what they enjoy, and they hire an assistant to do the rest. In love relationships, however, we're not always so smart about roles. We let tradition prescribe them—or we *fear* that tradition will—instead of approaching them as another area for joint decision.

Like being a highly sexual person or a giver or a homebody, your feelings about your role in a relationship are deeply entrenched and hard to change. So are his. If his idea of how you should hold up your end of a relationship differs greatly from yours—he calls it "love"; you call it "servitude"—he's not the Right One.

Roles can be treacherous if, like many women, you want a free ride—that is, you want the full benefit of equality without any of the costs, or you want all of the old protectionism *and* all of the new independence. That's like asking a man to go into business with you as equal partners—only you want him to put in all the money and take complete responsibility for the operation of the business and still share the authority and profits with you.

My dear, you can't have it both ways. In love, you really do get what you pay for. If you're looking for a man to assume full control of your standard of living and your economic future without any help from you, you'll have to trade down in power by assuming a traditional role. If you're willing to trade down in earning power for a man who has other attributes (see Joan and Tony in the previous chapter), you may have to finance that trade with some of your own money. The role you play in a relationship—the sum total of your obligations and rights— must always be seen in the context of a *reciprocal trade-off of costs* (giving up something in exchange for something else).

Among working women with ambitious career plans, there's a suspicion that no matter how well intentioned or flexible a man is, once you marry him, he'll subvert you into white slavery. The female commitmentphobe is like a macho man who's afraid of his tender "feminine" feelings and has to maintain a brittle facade of strength and competence. Often a workaholic, she's attracted to rejecting or inaccessible men and is wary of any who might detect and take advantage of her hidden vulnerability, which is not the weakness she imagines it to be, but the normal need for intimate love. Determined not to get locked into the role that consumed her mother, she pays her own bills, plans her own life, and leaves the cooking to someone else.

The rise of the "facho" woman (feminine macho) is a response to our confusion about roles. What facho women don't understand is that roles don't determine us; we determine them. In a good relationship, roles are as flexible and interchangeable (or as rigid and unchangeable) as the partners want them to

be. Saying the magic words *I do* to the Right One won't instantly shrivel you up and make you into an old crone who
wears aprons all the time. *You are not your mother.* (I know that's
not how she looked when you were growing up, but that's
how a facho friend once told me she pictured her mother in
secret horror.)

The corollary to the above is *All men are not your father.* Not
every man is a slave-king in disguise who has to sit down to
a sumptuous gourmet meal and be served and waited on when
you come dragging home from work. There *are* other options,
like restaurants and convenience foods (Marie Antoinette wasn't
kidding when she said, "Let them eat cake"), or his cooking.

True, the classic macho man, the *doyen* who wants his meals
home-cooked and his shirts hand-pressed, is still very much
with us. But you'd be surprised how many men there are—the
sharers—who'll gladly accept others kinds of gain (intellectual
stimulation, a financial contribution, sensitivity to their particular emotional needs) as a valid medium of exchange in love
and will respond by sharing the daily chores. At the top of
the scale, there's the "maretaker" (male caretaker)—a man who
actually enjoys cooking and attending to your other creature
comforts because he identifies with the maternal role (a rich
maretaker is second only to God).

Whether you're a caretaker, facho, or sharer type yourself,
you have a right to look for a man who's compatible with you.
To help you find that man, here's a list of the pairs that are
possible and their compatibility rating:

FEMALE		MALE		
Facho	+	Macho	=	Terrible
Facho	+	Sharer	=	Fair
Facho	+	Maretaker	=	Excellent
Sharer	+	Macho	=	Fair
Sharer	+	Sharer	=	Good

Sharer	+	Maretaker	=	Good
Caretaker	+	Macho	=	Excellent
Caretaker	+	Sharer	=	Good
Caretaker	+	Maretaker	=	Good

The Right One is drawing closer and closer now because at last you've identified him. He's someone who, if you could put a cross section of his center under a microscope, would have four areas that match up well with your own: sexuality, personality, life-style, and role. Remember, within each area there is a whole cluster of priorities that you can trade up or down on (or negotiate) to reach a favorable balance. You may have greater or lesser compatibility than you'd like in an area, but that's a difference in degree rather than kind.

If any one of his central areas matches up with yours like a rock on a trampoline, you're headed for trouble going into a long-term relationship with him. You might stay together, but that rock will never move. With two mismatched areas, you've got to have rocks in your head even to consider him.

Once you've found the Right One, you'll have to keep your eye on those four areas of compatibility to make sure they *stay* compatible. But don't fret—you'll be rewarded for your attentiveness with a relationship you thought women only wrote about in books.

Lifting the Lid

Now that you know what you're looking for underneath the surface attraction, how do you go about finding out what's there?

This is the part that takes skill and guts. You've got to have the courage to pursue the truth, and yet be subtle enough about it not to come off sounding like a prosecuting attorney. And you need that same combination of courage and editorial skill in telling *your* story—truthful enough not to be mislead-

ing, but not so truthful that you strip away the last shred of
romance.

Pretense in love is ultimately boring, or it wins you the
wrong one. There are two reasons why you might be tempted
to engage in pretense in a relationship: One is your fear of
losing the man by revealing things about yourself that are
unacceptable to him; and the other is your fear of losing the
man by learning things about him that are unacceptable to
you. You could be wrong about either one—or you could be
right.

If you're wrong, you have nothing to lose and everything
to gain by *gently* lifting the lid of superficial banter you're both
using to cover what you really need, enjoy, and think. At the
very first peek inside, your relationship will start to come alive
with more meaning and excitement for both of you because
you'll be discovering that you *can* accept each other's real self.
If, by lifting the lid, your fears are confirmed—there *is* some
basic incompatibility that neither of you can accept—the sooner
you know that, the better. You can still maintain the relationship if you want to, but you won't be in the dark anymore.
You've positioned yourself to take your losses early.

A certain amount of playacting is necessary in the initial
stages of a relationship to create an atmosphere of romance
and allure. But once the romance has jelled, you have to begin
lifting the lid little by little. Since men have been trained to
be the buyer in relationships, he'll probably be more outspoken
about what he needs in a partner. If he's the reticent type,
however, you may have to dig it out of him by questioning
him directly—"Let's talk here," as Joan Rivers says—about all
the things we've already discussed: his sexual attitudes, emotional needs, values, interests, etc.

Inviting him to go away with you for a weekend or on a
trip, where you can expand your range of shared experiences,
is a good way to move the relationship to a deeper level. (You
may never see him again after that, but you know what I told

you about taking your losses early.) In my own case, having the courage to ask Larry to join me in Miami when I was on tour with my last book was a turning point in our relationship. We'd been seeing each other only five months at that time, so it was either invite him to be with me midway through the tour or risk being apart for a month (a suicidal risk with a man in demand).

You'll never know how much nerve it took for me to ask him. I wasn't going to make it easy for him by throwing plane fare from Philadelphia to Miami into the deal (as I saw it, being together was the issue, not a free vacation). To my infinite delight, however, Larry not only accepted my invitation but arrived bearing the most imaginative and caring gift—a poster-size crossword puzzle based on my book, *Limits*. It had taken him fifteen hours to design it and staple it together, and it is now framed and hanging on the wall in the foyer of our home. The fruits of a well-taken risk are sweet indeed.

The reluctance of a facho woman to make herself vulnerable to a man by revealing her secret desires is twofold. It's prompted as much by the fear that he *will* accommodate her (and pull her away from her work) as by the fear that he won't. Susan, a soft-spoken but hard-nosed marketing manager who avoided commitment in a relationship for ten years until she married at the age of thirty-two, is typical. Her pattern was to abandon a relationship the moment the first blush of romance faded. "I was like a little girl chasing balloons," she recalls. "Men were crazy about me because I never said what I wanted; but when they weren't giving me what I wanted by reading my mind, I'd feel justified in leaving them."

And then Susan fell in love. This man was different from all the others—he wouldn't be content with pretense. He encouraged Susan to say what she wanted from him—and, by God, he was willing to give it to her! Now Susan was *really* scared. The exposure of her true self to a man, even though it was affirmed, made her more terrified of commitment than ever. But the vividness of her connection with this man—that "on all fours" feeling—propelled her to plunge into the river headlong. To her surprise (but not to mine), she hasn't been submerged. She's finding marriage to be not a restriction of her dreams but an impetus to achieve them—a discovery she never would have made if the Right One hadn't lifted the lid.

If he won't do it, take the initiative yourself and get beyond the pretense. Ask questions, probe, tell him how you feel, let him know who you are and what you want. Don't let the small talk, jokes, war stories, and all that other superficial dating dialogue keep you from being no more to each other than intimate strangers. If he's the Right One, to love him is to know him and be known by him as you really are.

The Boutique Theory

The secret of success in business is *repeat* business. No one ever went broke keeping the customers satisfied. The entrepreneurs who became millionaires all did it by discovering a need in the marketplace and filling that need better than anyone else— they built a better mousetrap.

The same principle applies to romantic success. Your Right One is a customer shopping for love. What can *you* give him that the competition can't? Why should he do business at your store and not at the woman's down the street? Which needs of his are you uniquely equipped to fill with your better mouse- trap? How are you going to keep him coming back for more?

I have an answer for you: my "boutique theory" of love. Think of all the goods and services that you have to offer the Right One, and you'll see that you're the owner of a specialty shop—not some ordinary supermarket with something for ev- eryone, but a *boutique* that happens to cater to this man's par- ticular needs and tastes in a relationship. You keep him coming back because you give him premier treatment. He can't find a

competitor of yours out there who's more in touch with what
he wants and delivers it so superlatively.

The owner of a boutique carries the right stuff for her customer—she has what he's really looking for—but she's also
clever about encouraging his taste in new directions and getting
him interested in other items in her inventory. And she always
insists on the right price: She lets him know what *she* needs
from *him*.

The boutique theory of love will help you understand why
you can't be all things to all men, and why satisfying the Right
One is a calling in itself. Your biggest challenge is to wear
down your customer's sales resistance. He comes to you wanting to buy, yet fearing that he'll be taken. But because you're
sensitive to what he needs, you're able to win him over by
aligning yourself with him and conveying your sense that he's
a very special person.

Creating a *special* relationship for the Right One is the es-
sence of the boutique theory. Whatever you give him—tenderness, good times, sex, a gift—it has to suit him perfectly,
but at the same time be distinctively yours. For example, you
know he loves jazz, but buying him a Dave Brubeck album is
too uninspired (that's the kind of thing the manager of a department store would do, not the proprietor of a boutique).
So without telling him about it, you hire a local group of
musicians and arrange for them to show up at his house one
night that you know will be convenient for him, to do a jam
session just for him!

Giving him perks—extras similar to the privileges or luxuries
that are used to sweeten business transactions, like an executive's having the use of a company car—can be extremely
persuasive. If you have perks coming to you through your work
or social contacts, share them with him.

One of the most captivating perks I gave Larry when we
were dating—a treat he wasn't likely to get from any of my
competitors—was a trip to the celebrated Broadmoor Hotel

in Colorado Springs. I'd been invited there to be a guest lecturer at a conference, and I was getting all expenses paid for two instead of a fee—as ideal a perk as you're likely to find. It had the word *special* stamped all over it. I still remember lying in the sun in a lounge chair while Larry was jogging around the Broadmoor's lake, a giant turquoise oval ringed with evergreens and stretching back to the magnificent hills of the Rockies. Even more spectacular was the reception we got the night we visited the Air Force Academy. We walked to the entrance down a red carpet between two rows of officers who stood at attention on either side and formed a shining steel canopy with their tilted swords. For sheer originality, that was hard to beat.

Be imaginative! Express your love for him with flair as well as sensitivity. How much money you spend isn't relevant— it's the giving of *you*. But don't be stingy either. Spring for an expensive dinner out occasionally and consider it one of the best investments you'll ever make (more men than you can shake a maître d' at want to be *treated* for a change). And never try to substitute something you want him to have for something he wants. A costly French dinner won't assuage a man's sexual appetite, and it doesn't answer his need for the kind of caring expressed by a home-cooked meal every once in a while. A perk isn't a replacement for your basic compatibility; it's an added attraction.

Your boutique quality of love should extend to a man's children and his other family members or friends who make up his circle of influence. Treat them with the same perception and caring as you treat him. Word-of-mouth recommendations (or criticisms) are not insignificant.

Although you may think it's a buyer's market in love today, the woman who's determined to build a better mousetrap has more of a capacity to attract the right customer and keep him satisfied than she realizes. What she must do is target her market, devote herself unstintingly to filling the set of needs that she can fill best, and always have the courage to ask her price. If she can do that, the ultimate reward will be hers: a lasting relationship with the Right One.

MORAL: You can't find the Right One unless you know who that is.
COROLLARY: Once you know he's right for you, never let him forget it.

8

Lovemanship: The State of the Art

*Y*ou're posed on the ladder of love on the landing between your last Dress Rehearsal and the Real Thing. After coming all this way, you don't want to blow it by slipping back into behavior that'll bring you down. Therefore, before you take that next momentous step onto the highest rung, let's pause for a moment and make sure you've got the basic principles of lovemanship down pat. While the laws of love don't operate on a mechanical cause-and-effect basis (if you say the magic words, he'll ask you to marry him), they are prescriptive. By giving you a handle on some basic truths about human nature, they can guide you away from failure and toward success.

This is what you paid your money for—the fundamentals that will help you pick the right person and perform like a champion. You've already encountered these rules in the stories and incidents I've related to you in the preceding pages. For your convenience, I've organized the most important insights into this handy little syllabus of lovemanship: my eight Laws of Love.

Law 1: One Rebound Begets Another

As we've learned from the singles-bar horror stories, it's an exercise in masochism to attempt a serious involvement with someone who hasn't healed from the breakup of a relationship. How well matched you are is immaterial here; to a man on the rebound, you're invisible except as an object to ease the pain, erase the memory, or prove a point about his virility. To protect himself from getting hurt again, he'll erect defenses against you that would have NATO drooling with envy. Don't let yourself be exploited by this man—cultivate him as a contact only.

If *you're* on the rebound, look for a friend rather than a quick replacement.

Law 2: Don't Open With an Act You Can't Follow

Running yourself ragged for him at the outset smacks of desperation and locks you into an untenable position that will backfire down the line. Quickly set limits on the amount of "sweat equity" you'll expend to make a go of your relationship. Your obligation to do the heavy lifting is no greater than his.

Law 3: Take Your Losses Early

Never surrender your power to act in your own behalf for fear of losing the man. The longer you defer a potential loss because you're afraid to negotiate for what you want, the bigger your investment in the relationship grows and the greater becomes the loss. Exercise your right to know the worst (or best) about him graciously—but do it early on. When an important issue is at stake (he's still in love with someone else; he can't change his bad habits, etc.), bucking the status quo is the preferred risk over inaction or appeasement.

Law 4: Don't Tell Him Anything He Shouldn't Hear

Edit out of your life story any damaging revelations that have no direct bearing on *this* relationship. Being straight with him about where you're coming from *now*—not where you've been—is the only kind of "openness and honesty" that's essential to a quality relationship. Don't wallow in self-disclosure to the point where you destroy your ideal image too quickly or rob your relationship of the kernel of mystery that lies at the heart of romance. Remember, who you are today is your gift to him, and think how the deliciously slow unwrapping of a gift is often the most exciting part.

Law 5: It's Better for Him to Think He Can't Mistreat You Than to Find Out He Can

You won't get the best out of a man unless you act as if you deserve the best. Once he thinks you'll accept his lowest offer, that's what he'll give you. Fostering the impression that he won't get away with shoddy behavior—calling you for dates at the last minute; frequently breaking dates; leaving you alone on holidays; buying you cheap, impersonal gifts; and other atrocities—may be enough to deter him from giving you the short end. But if he calls your bluff and tries to take advantage of you, you have to counter by refusing to accept his terms.

Otherwise, you've lost your bargaining position and won't regain it without a dogfight.

Law 6: Never Gamble with More Than You Can Afford to Lose

Exhausting your resources to win over a reluctant lover is like mortgaging your house for a single hand of blackjack. Give it your best shot, but don't blow your whole wad on someone who sets up extravagant demands as a precondition for getting serious with you ("Buy me a Maserati with your kids' college money and I'll love you"). Even if the demand is relatively benign, like insistence that you lose twenty pounds, *qualification* itself indicates a big downside risk (after you lose the weight, he'll find something else about you that's preventing him from falling in love). Losing twenty pounds if you're overweight is an affordable, even desirable, loss, but gambling with your "bread money" (psychological assets like self-respect are included here) is no more advisable in the game of love than it is in the casino at Monte Carlo.

Law 7: You Can't Dodge a Curve Unless You See It Coming

Keep alert to hidden soft spots—pressure from a rival, a drinking problem, financial reverses—so that trouble won't catch you by surprise. You can always handle a catastrophe better when you have advance notice.

Law 8: He Can't Catch You If You Never Run the Other Way

Nothing ignites a man's interest like a touch of intrigue. If you're constantly available to him during the chase, why should he want to pursue you? The smart woman knows how to leverage her options, even ones she's not actively pursuing, so that she subtly shifts the balance of power in her direction and, to use the age-old expression, "lets a man chase her until she catches him." *Using leverage in love* is such a vital part of your lovemanship repertoire that I've devoted the whole next chapter to a detailed elucidation of how to do it.

9

Using Leverage in Love

*L*uck, as a famous football coach once said, is when preparation meets opportunity. In the game of love, your ultimate opportunity presents itself when the Right One (you recognize him from reading chapter 7) finally enters your life. He's here! Will you be "lucky" enough to make the most of this glorious opportunity? That depends not on the whims of fate nor on the roll of some cosmic dice, but on *you*—how much you've learned from previous relationships, how well you've mastered the basics, how *prepared* you are to grab that ball out of the air and run with it into the end zone.

This is the chapter I've been waiting to write because it crystallizes everything I've had to say in this book about asserting your womanly power and strategizing for romantic success. Finding someone you could love forever is only half the battle; the other half is getting him to agree to it. The fact that he's right for you—and you for him—is no guaranty that he's ready to commit himself to you for a lasting relationship. Getting him to that point may well be the most critical test of your prowess. The strategy you use must be timely and appropriate—not ordinary pressure, but *leverage*. If you're fully prepared for the Right One, you'll find that using leverage in love (maximizing your options by dealing from strength) will come naturally to you and bring the results you've been dreaming about for years.

Let me clarify what I mean by "dealing from strength." When you come from the position that you're as valuable as he is and that you have as much right as he does to establish a relationship, end it, or influence its direction and overall quality—that, my friend, is dealing from strength.

It's not your outward style that determines strength but your conviction underlying it—your sense that *you're* in charge of what you're doing. Coercive bloodhound tactics, for example, aren't "strong," because they're grounded in a desperate lack of control that throws all the power to the pursued. Intimidating men when you mean to attract them isn't "strong" either, because your ambivalence is dominating your moves. Only when you're *managing* your objectives are you dealing from strength.

The neat thing about leverage is that you can use it even while you're scared to death, and it'll still bring terrific results. Very often, dealing from strength means that you're using leverage *in spite of* your fears and not because of them.

My friend Adele, a bank officer, provides a perfect example. A whiz at multinational investment deals, she was going crazy because her boyfriend, Ben, a prominent and very wealthy businessman, had women chasing after him like runners in the Boston Marathon (a fact Ben did nothing to hide). Ben called Adele one day to tell her that he'd accepted the invitation of a socialite friend to go to Europe with her for the weekend. Reassuringly, he made a date with Adele for the Monday night of his return. (Don't you love it?)

Adele called me, agonizing over this situation and begging me for advice. "You have to break the date with him," I told her, "and do it at the very last moment. Monday, before the close of business, have your secretary call him and cancel, explaining that you had to leave early to shop for a dress because a very important dinner engagement came up unexpectedly."

Adele was aghast, but I convinced her to follow my instructions. With great trepidation, she broke the date. She called me Monday night, very late, to tell me that she couldn't sleep and was worried sick that she'd never hear from Ben again. All day Tuesday, in cold sweats, Adele fought the Battle of Ma Bell, physically restraining herself from calling Ben to get back in his good graces. Then Wednesday came and—hallelujah, praise be to God—Ben called. Adele couldn't believe the timid note in his voice. He sounded like a little boy requesting a big favor: "Are you free *tonight?*"

Now *that's* using leverage. My broken-date ploy had shifted the balance of power toward Adele, making her a force to be reckoned with instead of some passive nebbish to be taken for granted.

"But that's *manipulation,*" you say in horror. Well, what if it is? Psychologists make a distinction between *benign* manipulation that's sincere and for a good purpose (making yourself more desirable to someone you genuinely care about, for example) and *bad* manipulation that's insincere or exploitative. I'm as horrified as you are by wiles that aren't true to a woman's deeper motives (I cringe when I think of yesterday's "total woman" conning a new refrigerator out of her husband with phony displays of desire). But when your motives are pure— you've found the Right One and desire is dancing to its own beat—it's the competition or the other barriers to love that you're trying to subvert, not the man. Considering what the competition and the barriers are like today, you've got to wield all the leverage at your command—and that includes a little benign manipulation.

Using leverage in love won't backfire on you if you exercise exquisite sensitivity to his needs. You can't fool around with ploys (or his emotions) arbitrarily and expect to achieve the desired results. Playing hard-to-get when he needs assurance will scare him off as surely as camping on his doorstep when he wants to be alone. Your objective is to draw him into an irresistible collaboration that provides each of you with the best of the old dependence and the best of the new independence and spares you the worst of either. You can't hit on the right strategies for accomplishing this goal unless you take your cues from what's going on in the relationship.

If he's the Right One, why, you may ask, is all this childish, cat-and-mouse game-playing necessary? It's necessary *because* he's the Right One. He's not any man; he's special. After all the growing you've done, you've found someone as desirable and selective as you are. This man knows that he has an abundance of options, and while that makes him intensely exciting, it doesn't make him easy to get.

Unlike the men in your Wellingtons and Half-Loaves—self-doubting men who were content to settle for the illusions of love and pour their energies into maintaining that fiction—the Right One has confidence in his lovability. And in the noblest sense of the word, love is a *confidence* game: It calls for repeated acts of bravery. Falling in love with the Right One means *growing* in love with him, testing each other out, chancing action and commitment as you go for ever-deepening levels of closeness.

The Option Bluff

"Doubt makes you try," a platonic once told me, explaining the thrill of the chase. His point was that without uncertainty, there's no challenge. Success that's handed to you leads to boredom. If you know you can have it without having to work for it, where's the incentive? In any endeavor, it's the tension between the difficulty of a task and your competence at it that engages you and makes accomplishment so rewarding.

Since certainty dulls a person's interest, the way to love anything is to realize that it might be lost. (I'd like to take credit for that one, but G. K. Chesterton said it first.) As a woman in a culture that has traditionally overvalued men, you're likely to be more loss-conscious than he is when you enter a love relationship, even with the Right One. Having someone probably doesn't represent the same "salvation" to him as it does to you; and if it does, the population tilt gives him a bigger safety net of replacements to fall back on in case you don't work out.

Culture and biology have saddled you with an unfair handicap, but you don't have to take it lying down. *Leverage is the great equalizer.* Although you may have fewer options than he does on the face of it, how many options you actually have isn't as important as his *perception* of them. By bluffing about your options, even fabricating a few if you have to, you can raise the ante and make him as worried about losing as you are. You're not practicing deceit to make a fool of him; you're doing it to put yourself on an equal footing. There's nothing immoral about jockeying for position. As long as you're not lying about your objectives (pretending to care for him when you don't; pretending you don't want a commitment when you do), bluffing is benign manipulation.

I've noticed that men are totally honest about their options only when it's to their advantage. Ben, for example, had no qualms about telling Adele that he was going away to Europe for the weekend with a woman who'd invited him. If the truth wouldn't have earned him points, he'd have said he was going to Europe on a business trip. (We're assuming he was telling the truth; maybe *he* was bluffing.)

Rarely, if ever, will a man who's interested in you lead you to believe that you're his only hope. If he doesn't come right out and tell you about the other women he's seeing (I'll get to how to handle that a bit later), he'll do it by implication. The hardball player will deliberately make sly references to clubs that he's been to recently or new ones that he's discovered just to let you know that he's not sitting home alone when you aren't around. Then he'll shrewdly observe your reaction for signs of jealousy, and he'll do nothing to correct any misconceptions you might have. He could have gone to those clubs with his sister and walked out with her five minutes later, but you'll never know (not unless you marry him and hold his heels to the fire).

Whether his provocation of jealousy is intentional or simply an outgrowth of the imbalance of power between the sexes, you have to show him that he has competition, too. I admit that this takes some ingenuity when he's got ten other women to juggle around and you're home painting your toenails on your off night, but leverage will save the day.

Let's return to Ben and Adele for a moment, and you'll see what I mean. Thrilled to hear from him after she'd broken their date, Adele eagerly accepted Ben's invitation to dinner that Wednesday night. Left to her own devices, she would have listened in misery to Ben's account of his European fling with the socialite and admitted that she'd spent a depressing weekend alone. (Adele was the kind of woman who had to be saved from herself.) But I prevailed on her to keep up the option bluff and coached her on how to do it. "If he asks you what you did while he was away," I advised, "tell him you went skiing in Stowe, Vermont."

"But I can't!" Adele squealed. "I've never gone skiing in my life. What if he asks me the name of the middle lift?"

"Tell him you're a beginner," I said.

Adele tried it, embellishing her story with a wealth of detail gleaned from a friend who'd been to Stowe. Afterward, she reported back to me gleefully on Ben's reaction: "His mouth dropped open and he sat there like a statue, just staring at me while the ash on his cigarette kept getting longer and longer."

Adele dazzled Ben by leading from strength. Instead of succumbing to jealousy on demand, she showed him that she was calling her own shots. Her implied message was "I'm not worried about losing you; I'll let you worry about losing me." The power tactics stopped soon after that, and they went on to establish a climate of trust.

This is a good place to point out that using leverage in love is often the most effective way to cut game-playing short; it's your *failure* to deal from strength with a gamester that will suck you into a prolonged bout of mutual intimidation. If he tries to push you around, push back—but do it *right*. Don't rise to the bait and respond predictably; answer with a tactic that will restore your self-respect and upgrade the relationship at the same time.

Like Ben, most men who deliberately provoke jealousy in a partner are doing it to test the relationship: Your suffering is the gauge of how much you care. Some have other motives— revenge, punishment, rewards, increased self-esteem. But whatever the reason, when you're being threatened with a rival, jealousy of that rival is your most predictable response. The cleverer move is to ignore the rival and respond with a tactic that makes *you* more desirable to the man.

Sometimes the best tactic, as I showed Adele, is to reply in kind. When a jealousy-inducer (or some other love thug) is bullying you with the clout of his mightier options, that's the time to fight fire with fire. If you yield to your fear of abandonment and reduce yourself to such demeaning ploys as tearful entreaties, temper tantrums, heart-to-heart talks, endless interrogations, or demands for exclusivity, you'll only drive him further away by making him feel guilty and trapped.

Such "intimate terrorism," in psychologist Michael Vincent Miller's descriptive phrase, usually results in a vicious standoff. His abandonment tactics evoke an engulfing response from you, which in turn brings on further abandonment tactics from him, and so on, until pretty soon you've painted each other into separate corners. The game-playing has become an end in itself and a substitute for genuine closeness. Better to risk taking your losses early than to get pulled into a long-drawn-out affair with no happy resolution in sight.

Suppose he's not an intimate terrorist but has innocently provoked your jealousy because, decent about it though he is, he's obviously dating others. Should you reply in kind then? Absolutely! Why? Because he's showing you that he has a need for space. Any engulfing tactic on your part will cause this man to withdraw. Again, the smarter move is to keep him off-balance with a convincing option bluff. Here's where your network, your platonics, your safe sex partners, and outright lying, if you must, can help you cope with uncertainty until a more propitious time.

There are occasions, I must point out, when replying in kind is the wrong tactic. Remember, the whole point of using leverage in love is to move the relationship toward fulfilling closeness, not away from it. When you're dealing with a commitmentphobe, a man who's trying to distance himself from you because he fears a deep and permanently exclusive involvement, you've got to take care not to do anything to magnify the distance between you. You have to act according to *your* objectives, not his. Reminding him of your other options is a smart move only when it's used to draw him closer to you by maintaining the "sharp edge" of desire or by allaying his fear of entrapment. But you shouldn't give him back a dose of his own medicine out of pure spite—hostile rivalry will only widen the gulf he's trying to create between you.

One of the commitmentphobe's favorite ploys, for example, is to talk about a previous relationship continually while assuring you that it's all over. Maybe it *is* all over (that's something you have to find out), but he's using it as a wedge between you. His compulsive allusions to it lack the Bleeding Heart's morbid breast-beating or the jealousy-inducer's playful malice. His intent is clearly to talk about *that* in order to avoid talking about the two of *you*. Don't fall into the trap and add to the barricade he's put up by blabbing about a previous relationship of yours in retaliation. Tell him, "When I'm with you, I want to be as fully with you as I can—give you all of my attention and not think about anyone else. Won't you do as much for me?"

If he can't honor this request, you know he's not for you. My friend Ellen once tried this ploy with Fred, an incurable commitmentphobe who brought out her worst insecurities. They were sitting around his pool one day, batting previous relationships at each other in a pointless contest, until Ellen finally had enough. She told Fred that she'd stop talking about Him if he'd stop talking about Her. Fred gave Ellen his promise, even shook hands on it, but soon lapsed into his same old "eulogy to the dead" routine. Wisely, Ellen took that as a signal to take her losses early and move on.

Ellen had occasion to use that same tactic again when she began seeing Brett, her current husband. Their relationship was rolling along, but not as merrily as it might have without Brett's compulsive "wifism"—a syndrome that afflicts many divorcing men who mourn the loss of a wife by deifying her and continually singing her praises. (The opposite syndrome among women—a common tendency to *downgrade* an ex-husband—suggests that men feel obliged to justify their choice of an ex-spouse, whereas women feel they have to explain why they didn't keep him.)

Although Ellen had Brett's repeated reassurances that his marriage to Gwen was kaput, his continual references to Gwen, in only the most glowing terms, made Ellen feel like a poor second. She sensed that her position would never improve as long as Brett kept invoking the Great Gwen for protection, but she was afraid to do anything about it. Finally, she was *shamed* into confronting him after some friends they'd gone on a trip with one weekend remarked to Ellen privately that there was "too much Gwen."

After their friends had left for home, Ellen was having a quiet drink with Brett in the hotel bar when she decided that the time had come to get Gwen off her back, for better or for worse. With infinite tact (delivering bad news with compassion reduces the risk of getting shot for it), Ellen told Brett what their friends had said about there being "too much Gwen" and followed that revelation with the Request for Undivided Attention tactic.

Brett was utterly crestfallen. He claimed that he hadn't been aware of hyping Gwen so much, especially in front of friends. It was only a habit, he insisted, and he could easily break himself of it with a little concentration.

"I thought Brett was underestimating the hold Gwen had on him," Ellen says, "but he fooled me. From then on, he never mentioned Gwen's name again except when it was really necessary." Ellen marvels even now at the beneficial effect that strategy had on their relationship: "We turned a corner and got much closer. I was the first woman who forced Brett to throw away his life raft. It was scary for both of us, but I never would have gotten anywhere with him if I hadn't made that initial breakthrough."

There's another time when you should resist the temptation to reply in kind to a commitmentphobe's distancing tactics, and that's at the outset when he tells you that he wants a relationship but isn't ready to settle down (we're talking about *curable* phobes here, having already learned to weed out the incurables for anything except fun and games). Don't try to gain his confidence by lying about your own objectives or subverting them to his. *Never commit yourself to noncommitment.*

Even if you're genuinely wary of commitment, don't preclude a possible change of heart. You can tell him about your reservations, but don't express them as absolutes ("I'll never trust a man"; "I'll never give up my freedom"; etc.). Those commitmentphobic buzz words give a man the license to enjoy you sexually without investing his emotions.

Given the female tendency to become attached through sex, your fear of commitment may dissipate when you realize that he's worthy of trust. You may find that you do want a committed relationship with him, after all—but how do you change the ground rules after the game has begun? By now, alas, he's got you classified as a "safe sex" partner or a buddy or just a good kid, rather than a potential Right One. And try as you may, you can't get him to change that classification any more than *you* can readily switch on passion for a platonic.

A commitmentphobic man has to be romanced out of his fears, not jollied out of them. An answering fear of commitment on your part will only reinforce his defenses. You must entice him with tempting vulnerability. Take the stance that, while you're not *looking* for a commitment, anything's possible with the Right One.

Buying Time

The rallying cry of the curable commitmentphobe is "I love you, darling, but I'm keeping my options open." Waiting for a man to make up his mind can be an agonizing experience— so agonizing, in fact, that the inability to tolerate delay is a leading cause of failure in love. Women who haven't mastered the art of using leverage to buy time with a foot-dragging lover often get maneuvered into an impetuous sudden-death tactic— a full-scale assault on a man that either extorts a commitment from him or kills the relationship.

Jennifer, a vivacious but hotheaded twenty-eight-year-old secretary, almost sank her own ship when she ran out of patience with Keith and impulsively made a sudden-death phone call to him one night. "I was sick and tired of being limited to every other weekend so he could continue seeing others," she explains. "It infuriated me to have to wait my turn in the rotation, but I never turned him down when he called me, because I loved being with Keith and thought I'd be cutting off my nose to spite my face. I used to dream about getting even with him if only I had somebody else. My favorite fantasy was that Keith would call me up to ask me out and I'd say, 'I'd love to, sweetheart, but I can't—I'm getting married.' "

So much for fantasies. The reality is that after six months

of swallowing her pride, something in Jennifer finally snapped. She came home from work on a Thursday night in a foul mood. Her boss had gotten on her nerves; she'd had a fight with another woman in the office; and a traffic jam had delayed her ride home for over an hour. After two glasses of wine, Jennifer began brooding about the weekend. She had a date with Keith for Sunday night, which meant that he was spending prime time—Saturday night—with one of the other women in his stable. It was more than she could bear. In a cold fury, Jennifer picked up the phone and dialed Keith's number.

"I had no idea what I was going to say to him," Jennifer says. "Calling him was such a spur-of-the-moment thing that I hadn't even organized my thoughts. I started out being sweet and reasonable, and pretty soon I was throwing zingers at him left and right. I told him he was dense and insensitive and treated me like a piece of ass, among other things. He got mad, but he tried to be nice about it. He said that I was one of the two women he'd ever considered living with or marrying in his thirty-two years, but he just wasn't ready for that yet. And he didn't know when he *would* be ready, either—it could take a year, two years, six months."

Jennifer had all she could do not to retort, "Listen, you creep, by the time you're ready, I'll be long gone!" She was incensed, but she also knew that she was playing a dangerous game of brinkmanship and could easily push the relationship over the edge, so she backed off. She told Keith that she understood his need for more time, and she apologized for losing her temper. Then she made a very carefully worded statement of her intention to deal from strength. "I said something to the effect that since Keith was looking out for himself, I'd have to look out for myself, too," Jennifer recalls. "I wanted him to know that I wasn't going to sit around on the shelf anymore while he was doing his thing."

Unknowingly, Jennifer had stumbled onto the secret of how to make waiting tolerable: She *stopped* waiting. Instead of marking time when Keith wasn't with her, accumulating resentment like mold on stale bread, she began enjoying the time and letting Keith know she was enjoying it. Time became her ally now, rather than the enemy, and she found that, with leverage, she'd purchased a new lease on the relationship.

Goaded by her phone call into a more effective strategy, Jennifer decided to stop brooding over the weekend and do something about it. It happened to be July Fourth weekend, and instead of torturing herself with visions of Keith making fireworks with someone else, she bought two tickets to *Amadeus* and invited a platonic to see it with her. (The one redeeming social value holidays have is that they're the only times when you can get tickets to hit Broadway plays.) The platonic reciprocated by taking Jennifer to Sardi's after the show.

Sunday, when Keith showed up at her door, Jennifer was all aglow. She couldn't stop talking about Tim Curry's marvelous performance as Mozart the night before and about all the celebrities she'd spotted dining in Sardi's afterward. The barbecue Keith had gone to sounded terribly dull in comparison. As for the sexual fireworks, if any, who cared? Jennifer figured they couldn't have meant very much, judging by Keith's red-hot performance with her later that night.

After a marked upturn, Jennifer's relationship with Keith hit another snag. Once again he'd maneuvered her into a second-fiddle position to accommodate another woman he was seeing, and Jennifer had to use leverage to regain the first chair. "It was a Tuesday night," Jennifer remembers, "and we were lying in bed at his place after making love, feeling very warm and close. My mind drifted toward the weekend. Assuming we'd be together, I asked him what he wanted to do. He blurted guiltily, 'I have a dinner party Saturday night.' "

Unh! Jennifer felt as if Keith had whomped her in the gut with his knee. Whether his "dinner party" was real or a polite way of saying that he had a date, the rejection was the same. Jennifer's first instinct was to get out of bed and leave, putting an end to her anguish by aborting the relationship. But she controlled herself and said agreeably, "Let's make it Sunday night then, and I'll cook dinner at my place." Stunned by her generosity, Keith accepted.

Jennifer had bought time, and she put it to good use. She spent that whole Saturday preceding her date with Keith at her girlfriend Sandy's pool, soaking up the sun (it was August now) and acquiring a luxurious tan. She went to the movies with Sandy Saturday night, slept over at her apartment, and got out to the pool again Sunday morning to put a finishing bronze on her suntan. Then she dashed home, whipped up an elegant gourmet dinner for Keith, and set it off with her best linen tablecloth, good china, crystal stemware, and candlelight (Jennifer was not untutored in the basics of personal packaging).

The first thing Keith noticed when he arrived for dinner was Jennifer's splendid tan. He was all agog when she explained that she'd just gotten back a couple of hours ago from a jaunt on a friend's cabin cruiser (Sandy had been on a boat once and had raved about it to Jennifer at the pool). It took monumental discipline for Jennifer, but she banished all thoughts of Keith's activities the night before and concentrated solely on the here and now. Determined to give Keith a night he'd never forget, Jennifer was, by turns, doting, playful, clever, caring, passionate—a combination of earth mother and earth mover. It worked. Before long, she found that she'd been reinstated as Keith's Saturday-night date—a just reward for her patient persistence.

There were several other occasions when Jennifer's resourceful control over her impatience narrowly averted disaster. Finding herself alone on Thanksgiving because Keith wasn't ready to bring her home to his family in Cleveland, Jennifer spent the holiday with a "safe sex" partner who lent new meaning to the word *thanksgiving*. Another time, miffed at a recurrence of a Saturday-night "dinner party" for Keith, Jennifer announced that she was going to Atlantic City for the weekend on a gambling spree with a "friend" (the indispensable Sandy). She was amused to find three messages from Keith—count 'em, *three*—waiting for her on her answering machine when she returned late Sunday night.

All in all, Jennifer figures that she bought some eight crucial months of time from July Fourth until her engagement to Keith in March. Her severest test came at the end, during what Jennifer refers to now as the Nine-Day War. Keith took off for his "last hurrah" to the Cayman Islands, where he wanted to do some scuba diving and wrestle with the last vestiges of his commitment phobia.

Jennifer hunkered down for a hard time. Just when she thought she was going to break from the uncertainty, George, a former date who'd moved away to San Francisco, miraculously reappeared in her life. A dashing older man, George had come east for his daughter's wedding—a society bash that was being held on a five-acre estate in Tarrytown belonging to the groom's family. George asked Jennifer to be his date at the wedding, and she accepted without hesitation. Flattered by this signal honor, she also recognized it as the master stroke of leverage that she needed with Keith.

The wedding had those exotic flourishes that stick in the mind and make for a riveting tale. The service was held in a hunting lodge that had been converted into a chapel for the affair, and above the bridal canopy, staring out impassively at the seated guests, hung the huge, antlered head of a stuffed moose. Wait till I tell Keith *this*, Jennifer thought. The ceremony was followed by a lavish dinner in the mansion on the estate. Jennifer enjoyed every moment of her role as the father-of-the-bride's date, rekindling her affection for George as a friend without ending up in bed with him at the end of the evening.

"There were only a few days left until Keith would be back," Jennifer remembers, "and I couldn't wait to see him again. I was praying that he hadn't met someone else. I half expected him to say that he needed more time, but I knew it would put ideas in his head when he heard that a man had taken me to his daughter's wedding."

That it did. The day after Keith returned and was hit with Jennifer's member-of-the-wedding story, he proposed.

Romanticists will insist that Keith wouldn't have proposed to Jennifer if he didn't love her—and they're right. Love, however, takes time to grow, particularly when you're dealing with a commitmentphobe whose fears of entrapment or betrayal through intimacy are greater than most men's. Jennifer *was* the Right One for Keith, but their relationship might never have lasted long enough for him to find that out if she hadn't dropped her confrontational tactics and settled on a strategy geared toward buying time.

Dealing with the commitmentphobe is a formidable problem for women in this era of postrevolution fallout. If I'd followed the advice a psychiatrist friend gave me when I was going through this problem with Larry in his wild-oats stage—"Tell him to have his fling and get back to you when he's finished"— I'd still be single today (as the psychiatrist is, by the way, eight years after her divorce).

Mind you, I would defend unto death your right *not* to deal with a commitmentphobe if you don't want to. You certainly have the option to exclude from your list of potential partners any man who is actively engaged in playing the field and is reluctant to stop. But be advised that exercising that option will leave you with an exceedingly small list.

My point is that you *can* win with a phobe, provided he's not too far gone or too soon terminated. Patience with him is more than a virtue; it's a necessity. As we've seen, the commitmentphobe's moves are maddening: He insists on engaging in multiple relationships; he limits the number of times he'll see you; he talks constantly about his ex-wife or other relationships; he backs away the moment you come on strong.

Are these the symptoms of a hopeless case? That you must determine with time and the right tactics.

Set an internal deadline for gaining the commitment you want (details follow), and pace yourself accordingly. No matter how much you might want to kiss him off in a fit of pique during this time—*don't*. If you abandon the commitmentphobe prematurely, you've lost your edge to the competition. You can't take it personally that he wants to try others on for size. Concentrate on proving that *you* fit better than anybody else. *Maintain contact.* Use every waking (and sleeping) moment with him to build his trust, give him pleasure, and engage him emotionally.

Be aggressive and tough it out when he's pursuing the competition. If necessary, "scoop" the other woman by inviting him to something special Saturday night, and try to lock up the holidays with him far in advance. Like Jennifer, *fight back* if you find he's maneuvered you into being the weekday date while he's reserving weekends for her. Go off on some romantic toot (or pretend that you have), and throw him off-balance by telling him what a fantastic time you had. As long as you've done your homework, fake options are as serviceable as real ones. Create credible options however you can, and impress upon him that you're keeping them open while he is—*for a limited time only.*

How to Close

Although it's devoutly to be hoped that he'll come around of his own accord while the meter is still running on your deadline, you may have to apply some real pressure to elicit a commitment from him, even, as a last resort, breaking off relations with him. Here, timing is everything.

A real-estate salesman who became a millionaire in his twenties once told me that there's a "magic moment" for closing deals. If you ask for a commitment too soon, before you've sold the client on your product, you may be inviting a rebuff. If you talk *past* the point when the client has been sold, which happens far more often than jumping the gun, the sale will be *surely* lost because it's almost impossible to reactivate desire once it has waned.

Since intimate relationships put more of *you* on the line than most business deals do, you're especially prone to botch selling a man on commitment by pushing too soon or stalling the close too long. Again, you must go with the flow—move in concert with the rhythm of your particular relationship to sense that "magic moment" to close.

While the dynamics vary for each couple, there are certain general parameters you ought to consider. Research has shown that the "in love" phase for a romantic couple lasts anywhere from six months to two and a half years. But the average relationship today lasts only six months because women don't know how to use leverage to buy time. Where there's a conflict over commitment, it's not uncommon for a relationship to endure for four or even six years, often with turbulent ups and downs until the conflict is resolved one way or another. The most successful resolutions are always achieved by women who are clear about what they want and not afraid to fight for it in a timely and forthright manner.

I've seen enough tragedies to convince me that the mistake women most often make in closing is the *failure to deal from strength.* The "preemies" who can't wait out the obligatory six-month grace period often abort good relationships with their premature pressure. Many others—the "fence sitters"—*never* ask for a commitment or summon the courage to act on an internal deadline. They simply go along with the man's plans and objectives, feeling increasingly used and exploited, until they're reduced to delivering an ultimatum way past the point where it could possibly be effective.

The right time to ask for a commitment is *before* the "in love" phase peaks. Once that phase has crested and the bloom is off, the "magic moment" has passed. Let's look at the parameters again. You have six months for the relationship to jell and two and a half years at the outside to close it. That's the deadline period for a fairly intense relationship with frequent contact. Not having ready access to each other could extend your deadline period by as much as another year or so—but no one has forever.

After six months, set a deadline for broaching the subject of commitment. Weigh all the relevant factors in your relationship—age, career concerns, finances, family obligations, emotional state—and try to be reasonable about it. But if you can't be reasonable, be arbitrary. *An arbitrary deadline is better than none at all.* Courage is often discipline in disguise.

Somewhere between a year and eighteen months is usually the optimum time for a deadline because you have to allow an additional six to twelve months in case he asks for an extension—but let him ask. Think of it as being like the hour of giving birth—a time you can neither shrink from nor delay. When that time approaches, regardless of the terrors it holds, *deal from strength.*

I know it takes the utmost heroism to ask a man, and you should always *ask* what he wants to do rather than demand, "Will you stop seeing other women?" or "Would you like to live with me?" or "Are we ever going to get m-m-married?" (I guarantee you that word will stick in your throat.) Yes, asking is hard, but it's harder for him than it is for you. Whether it's rejection he's afraid of or entrapment, consider it all in a day's work if you have to help him out.

Asking for a commitment in due time is intelligent risk-taking at its finest. Maybe you'll lose him, but you can't help but lose him if you never speak up. Going silently down the path of least resistance will inevitably lead you past your "magic moment" toward the sudden death of the relationship or its demise through slow attrition.

Once you start negotiating for a commitment, always use a collaborative approach rather than a dogmatic all-or-nothing ultimatum. Talk in terms of feelings, not timetables: How does he feel about a committed relationship with you? Is one at all possible? How much time does he think he'll need? Question him about his feelings without trying to manipulate them. This may be the supreme test of your self-control. Resorting to engulfing tactics—tears, threats, accusations—may set you back irreparably at this juncture because he'll interpret such an assault on his initiative as emasculating. A lioness who's trying to prove she's tame doesn't roar and bare her claws.

Let's assume that after your first dialogue about commitment, you've come away with nothing worse than the request for additional time that you've already anticipated. Like Jennifer, you can use that time to help his love for you grow without a feeling of pressure. But if he's more resistant than Keith (or you've used the wrong tactics), you may find it necessary at the end of your deadline period to break off relations as a bargaining tool.

Never issue an ultimatum that sounds like an ultimatum. The trouble with either/or language—"either a committed relationship or none at all"—is that it locks you into a powerless position. The ball is in his court, but he can't throw it back to you without a wimpish surrender, and you can't get it back without an undignified loss of face. What if he doesn't surrender and you'd still like to see him? Resuming relations with him at that point is an admission of defeat.

You can achieve the same effect as an ultimatum without its crippling restriction of power by simply suggesting a separation. Tell him that you need time to think things over and to pursue your other options without guilt. You'd be surprised how many men come around with this kind of nonultimatum ultimatum. Missing you unbearably during your absence or suffering a nasty rejection (not *everyone* loves him the way you do) could literally bring him to his knees with a proposal of marriage.

Kim, a pert little hair stylist I know, had been involved for three years with her divorced boyfriend, Charlie, who drove her crazy because he insisted on playing the field. Kim still lived with her parents, and Charlie had his own apartment. She remembers driving over to his apartment one night when he had an assignation with a married woman he was seeing. Kim waited in the lobby until the other woman left, actually brushing past her on the way out, and then charged up to see Charlie.

"He came to the door all rumpled and sleepy," Kim says, "and I rushed into the bedroom where he'd just made love to *her*. I was so furious I couldn't see straight. Then I broke down and cried and cried and cried. It was awful. Charlie sat on the bed and held me while he wiped the tears from my cheeks and said, 'I'm sorry, Kim, but I don't love you.' "

Realizing the futility of her crying jag (I warned you about tears, didn't I?), Kim told Charlie, "Look, I really can't take this anymore. I think it would be best if I stopped seeing you for a while and began dating others. Let's see what happens." Then she left. Out on the street in the rainy night, she passed Charlie's car and, as a parting gesture, snapped his windshield wiper off in her hand.

Would it surprise you if I told you that a month after that maudlin scene Charlie called Kim and resumed the relationship? What's more, he resumed it *on her terms*. He stopped seeing others. He became more attentive to Kim's needs—sending flowers, complimenting her more often, buying her romantic gifts. And, yes, before they set a date for the wedding, he would say to Kim many times over, "I love you."

Now, you may ask, why did Charlie tell Kim he *didn't* love her on the eve of their separation? Because he was *afraid* to love her while she was constantly invading his turf, trying to manage and control his emotions. Men have an incredible capacity for self-protection. As much as you may arouse a man's passion, you won't arouse his love until you prove to him that you love him enough to let him be himself.

A separation doesn't always precipitate a marriage. It may end the relationship, permanently or cause it to be resumed on a purely platonic or "safe sex" basis. That's the chance you take when you go for the brass ring (make that gold with diamonds); but if you didn't attempt to close by the end of your deadline period, the relationship would fade into history anyway.

Here's another possibility. You may find when you reconcile after a separation that he's willing to live with you on an exclusive but unmarried basis. Think twice before you say yes. Don't get into this kind of arrangement unless you feel comfortable with it as a permanent way of life, because it may very well become one. You can indeed live happily ever after with him, but not if you're a strict traditionalist who needs the legitimacy or security of a marriage contract (that "little piece of paper from City Hall" *does* make a difference for most of us).

One of my friends who turned down the offer of a formal living-together arrangement succeeded in getting the marriage offer she wanted. Of those who accepted the arrangement, some tried it for a while and either got married or went their separate ways; others grew accustomed to not being married and will probably go on being happily unmarried to each other the rest of their lives. Permanence is guaranteed by the soundness of a commitment rather than its legality. The real issue is whether he's genuinely in love with you and capable of sharing his life with you in a satisfying way.

How can you tell? Analyze his objections to marriage carefully. Is he afraid of being swallowed up by the relationship? Afraid you'll change? Afraid he'll get bored? All of these are legitimate fears of entrapment, but they will recede as the relationship survives continued testing and you both find a workable balance between being private individuals and a couple.

But if his fears go to the heart of your connection—he's afraid you're too aggressive or too passive for him; too career-minded or too dependent; too materialistic or too much a free spirit—you may have a problem that commitment won't cure. Fearing intimacy more than we do, men are often more objective about the possibilities for failure. Then again, they're often hypersensitive to the experience of failure, too, like the cat that got burned on a hot stove lid and will never sit down on a hot stove lid again—or a cold one either. Hear him out, and go with your deepest convictions. Living with him is the right decision if you believe in the essential validity of the relationship regardless of a marital commitment.

Marriages that evolve out of a long struggle toward commitment are usually very successful. Trust has been accomplished without the sacrifice of romance. In the process of working through their conflicts together, the partners have arrived at a deeper understanding and appreciation of each other and, miraculously, are still in love. As Jack, a man who fiercely resisted commitment at first and is now happily married, puts it: "The new-wave romance is a second chance."

Jack met Lillian at a wedding in Los Angeles. She was twenty-five; he was twenty-three. When Lillian went to graduate school in San Diego, where Jack lived and had his printing business, she looked him up. They started dating and soon entered a sexual relationship. Jack was Lillian's fantasy guy: very romantic, old-fashioned, classy, intelligent, sensitive, well bred. There was only one problem—Lillian was ready for commitment and Jack wasn't.

Lillian remembers not hearing from Jack for days at a time. Compelled to drive by his home, she would go in, only to have Jack tell her that he wanted to be by himself. Lillian wouldn't leave. A devoted remedial reading teacher whose stubbornness worked well with her students but not with recalcitrant men, Lillian was determined to make Jack see the light. "I was infatuated with him," she says. "Jack was everything I wanted in a man. But I also thought there was so much more he could be doing with his life, and I wanted to help him achieve it."

Lillian wanted an exclusive relationship with Jack, but he wasn't interested. They went to parties together, and when he paid attention to other women, there were violent confrontations. Says Lillian: "Our first New Year's Eve together, after I caught him flirting with a friend, I went berserk. I got him out in the hall, grabbed him by the neck, and actually began choking him. It was a playacting kind of thing, just to say, 'You're really disappointing me.' But I left the party by myself."

On New Year's Day, a turning point occurred. Lillian drove over to Jack's house to help Donna and Barry, friends of theirs who'd been staying with him temporarily, move. "I dreaded facing Jack after making such a scene," Lillian recalls, "but I went upstairs and apologized. He apologized, too. We stood there, making these strained and awkward apologies, being terribly polite, and I thought to myself, This is what it's like when you give up."

It wasn't Jack Lillian gave up, only her determination to get him. They continued to see each other, spent a lot of time together, and became closer and closer in spite of Lillian's feeling deep down that it would never work out. "Spiritually there was a tie," Lillian says. "I had to be with him even though I knew he wasn't ready to settle down. It was agony for me. I was never without this horrible pain in the pit of my stomach. Going out with friends or with guys didn't alleviate the pain, but being occupied kept it away."

The better Lillian got to know Jack, the more certain she became that he was at a dead end in his work. She convinced him to sell his business and invest the money in a long filmmaking project. Over the next several years, they remained close but uncommitted. While Jack was learning a new profession, Lillian was also growing, deriving increasing satisfaction from her work and her circle of friends.

There were other men in Lillian's life, but since she had them pigeonholed as friends, she couldn't see any of them as a potential husband. This, she now realizes, was a mistake. "A favorite buddy of mine was my next-door neighbor, Russ, a charming guy who was a great person and a lot of fun," Lillian recalls. "I appreciated Russ, but I thought he was too low-brow for me, a carouser who didn't have Jack's class. And then my best friend, Frannie, fell in love with Russ after we dropped in on him one night and found him playing on the floor with his little nephew who had cerebral palsy. That made me think. Frannie's image of Russ was totally different from mine because in all the time that I knew him, I couldn't even *see* him."

Lillian learned never to pigeonhole men again. She began to understand the shifting nature of relationships: A man never changes his essential nature, which must always be seen realistically; but the way you relate to him can change, provided you haven't typecast him in bronze. (Men typecast, too, which is why I cautioned you against assuming the hard-boiled role of *"just* a friend" with a man who has the makings of the Right One.)

It was Jack who proved to Lillian that a man can go from being a potential husband to being a friend and back to a potential husband again. His documentary completed, he lined up a job with a commercial film company in New York and asked Lillian to follow him there and live with him. "I was reluctant to give up a good job and relocate without a total commitment on his part," says Lillian, "but I loved him too much to say no. My gut feeling was, 'Don't be a fool—go with it.' "

At his going-away party on his last night in San Diego, Jack spent the whole time flirting with blondes. Lillian was outraged. She believed Jack loved her and was only toying with the others, but she was through with being taken for granted.

Determined not to spoil what she thought would be their last time together, she stayed with him after the party and made love.

In the morning, as Jack was leaving, he said, "I'll call you when I get there." Very quietly, Lillian told him, "Don't bother." Her eyes met Jack's uncompromisingly, and she saw the look of recognition on his face. It had, after all, been *four years.*

En route to New York by car, Jack called Lillian some ten times. She refused to take his calls. Finally, when he arrived in New York and called again, she relented. "I love you very much for many reasons," Jack told her, "not the least of which is how much you love me and have been good to me all these years."

Lillian relented. She agreed to live with Jack in New York as soon as her teaching contract was up in nine months. After flying out to see him, she came home secure in the knowledge that Jack was fully committed to her.

Devising ways to fill the time until she could be with Jack permanently wasn't a trial for Lillian, because she already had a network of female friends and male platonics to keep her busy between her periodic visits to New York. With her girlfriend Nan, and Bill, a platonic who'd recently come off a relationship with a woman ten years older and was cooling out, Lillian formed a troika known as "The Three Musketeers." They went everywhere together—sailing, dancing, to the beach. Lillian will be forever grateful for their comradeship. "Nothing is better when you're in a situation like that," Lillian says, "than to have fun platonic relations with men who understand and respect where you're coming from."

When her contract expired, Lillian moved to New York to live with Jack, and they were married within a year. Lillian sums it up nicely: "When the man you love isn't ready to settle down, you have to decide whether he's worth waiting for. If you think he is, then you have to commit yourself to proving conclusively to him that your love is worth preserving forever."

Lasting love is not something people fall into—it's a conscious decision. It's an especially fearsome decision for men and women today because the hallmark of our time is a new appreciation of the value of personal freedom. Rather than risk getting sucked into the constrictive roles of the past, many prefer being alone or hopscotching from one short-term relationship to the next.

Although increasing numbers of facho women now fear the loss of autonomy as much as commitmentphobic men, the fear of engulfment is understandably greater for the New Man than it is for the New Woman. Psychologically, the male is the endangered species. He's the one being asked to give up his traditional defenses: control over the loved one and emotional detachment. Feeling threatened by the possible loss of self in a relationship of equals, the New Man has erected the escapist defense of the perennially open option.

There's no remedy for the dread of commitment—his or yours—other than the slow building of trust. The minimum requirement that induces any of us to entrust our soul to someone who knows us intimately is the confidence that this person won't hinder our development or take advantage of our vulnerability. That's the very least we need to have. As trust grows in a good relationship, the conviction arises that this person knows and affirms us as we really are and is committed to helping us become what we'd really like to be. That's the ultimate. If you have this deeply held conviction about the man you love and can inspire it in him *honestly*, romantic success is virtually guaranteed.

Make no mistake about it—men want a stable, satisfying, one-to-one relationship as much as we do. But since commitment spells more danger for them, there's a good chance that the burden of proof as to the merits of permanence in a viable relationship will fall on you.

Once you've identified the Right One, you can't be deterred by his persistent testing of the relationship. Don't quit in disgust when he makes a pretense of not caring as much as you intuitively sense he does or as much as his actions indicate. (Some men are so good at self-protection that they can be hooked before they're even aware of it.) His insistence on seeing others or even his denying that he loves you may be part of the elaborate defense system he's erected against a lasting involvement.

Give yourself ample time (but not too much) to prove to him that you're committed to loving him as anyone wants to be loved—in a way that doesn't diminish his possibilities for the future, but augments and enhances them. To be both autonomous and deeply committed to another is the true measure of romantic success. Your achievement of this success will derive, in the final analysis, from your perception and use of your own power to effect an irresistible quality of love.

MORAL: The way to a man's heart is through his cover.
COROLLARY: For those who know how to love both wisely *and* well, the way to a man's heart is always open.

The Last Word

*N*ow you know. Every woman *can* be adored, because the achievement of love is like any other achievement in life: It's the reward for a job well done. And any woman—even one not blessed with beauty, wealth, or brilliance—can perform like a champion at love by applying herself to the job and making the most of her options. Whether she *will* be adored is not up to the grace of God or the random kindness of a stranger. It's up to her.

More important than the strategies and techniques advanced in this book is the philosophy of love I've taught you. Always deal from strength and come from a position of self-respect. Never be afraid to risk losing the man sooner than suffer the loss of your power to act in your own behalf. And above all, prepare yourself for love by leading the kind of life that invites the right man into it and induces him to stay.

The wondrous thing about climbing the love ladder is how beautiful the view is along the way. Every relationship, no matter how it ends, helps shape your life and leaves a legacy of precious memories. That's what Tennyson meant when he said it's better to have loved and lost than never to have loved at all. But the plain truth is that to have loved and *won* is even better.

Why not find out for yourself?